THE SHOOTING SCRIPT®

THE
KING'S
SPEECH

THE KING'S SPEECH

SCREENPLAY AND INTRODUCTION BY
DAVID SEIDLER

NHB Shooting Scripts
NICK HERN BOOKS • LONDON
www.nickhernbooks.co.uk

This book first published in Great Britain in 2011 as an original paperback
by Nick Hern Books Ltd, The Glasshouse, 49A Goldhawk Road, London W12 8QP,
by arrangement with Newmarket Press, New York.

A CIP catalogue record of this book is available from the British Library.

ISBN 978-1-84842-183-7

THE NHB SHOOTING SCRIPT SERIES

The Actors
Adaptation
A Beautiful Mind
Being John Malkovich
Big Fish
Capote
Cinderella Man
Erin Brockovich
Eternal Sunshine of the Spotless Mind
The Good Shepherd
Gosford Park
I Went Down
The Ice Storm
In Good Company
Margot at the Wedding
Saltwater
The Shawshank Redemption
Slumdog Millionaire
The Squid and the Whale
Synecdoche, New York
The Truman Show
United 93

For information on forthcoming titles, please contact the publisher:
Nick Hern Books, The Glasshouse, 49A Goldhawk Road, London W12 8QP
e-mail: info@nickhernbooks.demon.co.uk

CONTENTS

CONTENTS

INTRODUCTION

DAVID SEIDLER

The crackle of the radio always got me excited. I loved that radio. The case was made of wood. Bakelite, as plastic was called, was too fancy for a lad. My wooden radio had holes in it. I'd been given a toy drill for Christmas. Never give a drill to a small boy unless you want holes in everything.

The static, like an overture, readied me for the thrills to come. If I'd been particularly well behaved it might be an American favorite, *Burns and Allen, Jack Benny,* or *Bob Hope.* This was an extra special occasion…the King was speaking tonight.

I remember his voice, high, and tense, with occasional pauses and hesitation. Yet the cumulative effect was marvelous: stalwart, staunch, and stirring. Despite his stutter he was able to deliver glorious sentences that rallied the free world. He was *my* King (I felt so proud of being British), and although everyone in the world, ally and enemy alike, listened critically to every syllable he uttered, he doggedly persevered.

So there was hope for me.

How I got to this point was a bumpy path.

Thud… My father Bernard and my uncle Sigmund were painting a sandbox for me, a happily spoiled only child. We were living in Lingfield, near the Surrey coast, which was probably a wise thing; during the Blitz an incendiary bomb crashed through the ceiling of the London apartment we had left at the start of hostilities.

I was less than three years old. *Thud…* The distant guns of Dunkirk. That was my first memory.

Reprinted by permission of the *The Mail on Sunday* (U.K.). ©2010 by Associated Newspaper Ltd.

Without explanation, in early 1940, my life changed completely. Like many middle-class children of that era, I'd seen little of my parents, being raised by a nanny. I adored Adelaide, with her halo of curly hair. She kissed me goodnight, telling me she'd always watch over me, yet in the morning she was gone.

Abruptly, we boarded a ship filled to the gunnels with folk like ourselves. Invasion was considered imminent. The Government was trying to relocate as many children as possible; I was one of the lucky ones, traveling with my parents. Requirements were stringent: the head of the household had to be exempt from service and able to earn a living outside the UK. My father had been in WWI, and as a fur broker who bought bales of pelts on commission, he had an office in New York City. We were on the list.

Off went the convoy of three ships, two filled with families, one with Italian POWs from North Africa. German U-boats sank one of the ships. Wrong one from their point of view. The Italians were locked in the holds. All perished.

My second memory is the Statue of Liberty.

On the voyage my stuttering began.

Childhood for those who stammer is not pleasant. You live in self-imposed silence because it is too painful to speak. Hard not to notice how uncomfortable everybody becomes: eyes glaze over, fingers tap, they want to get away as quickly as possible. Or try to be helpful, which is even worse. "Take your time…slow down…relax." If only it were that simple.

There was hope though. I heard it on my Swiss cheese radio. My parents told me, "The King was far worse than you." George VI of England, known as Bertie, gave inspiration to a little boy exiled to a former colony.

As I grew older I discovered telling lies was grand fun and decided to become a writer. My first attempt was *The Adventures of a Penny* as it traveled from hand to hand. I further resolved one day I'd write something about *my* King. I had no idea what.

It wasn't until university days when I first put my mind to it. That organ, however, was easily distracted by co-eds, so nothing much came of the effort.

Twenty years later I arrived in Hollywood, at the ripe age of forty, which is when most sane writers are leaving youth-oriented Lalaland. Fools however go where angels do not. My first job was writing *Tucker: The Man and His Dream* for Francis Ford Coppola. I naively thought this would change my life instantly (took ten years to get made) and I could then write anything I desired (which isn't quite the way it works).

So, being foolish and forty, I got on with it, reading every book about Bertie I could find. I didn't know what, in terms of a story, I was looking for, but I kept noticing little blips on the radar screen adding up to the question: *Who was Lionel Logue?*

Not a great deal was written about His Majesty's speech therapist, Lionel Logue, certainly not in the official biographies. Nor was much published about the royal stutter; it appeared to be a source of profound embarrassment. Today we've come a way in our dealings with the handicapped, but in Bertie's era the President of the United States Franklin Delano Roosevelt was never photographed standing, nor even sitting without his polio-stricken legs being discreetly covered with a blanket. A shriveled leg was a sign of weakness. So was a stammer. Those were the days when it was called a *defect*. You had a speech *defect* and thus you were a *defective* person. No wonder the royals swept it under the carpet.

Yet something, I've no idea what, writer's instinct I suppose, told me Logue was the story I was looking for.

I asked a friend in London to do a bit of detective work. I think that consisted of looking in the telephone directory. It produced the name and address of a surviving son of Lionel's, Dr. Valentine Logue, an eminent retired Harley Street brain surgeon. (In *The King's Speech* film he's the lad with his nose buried in textbooks.)

I wrote to him—this was in 1981, long before emails—and he replied if I came to London he'd be pleased to talk with me and even show me the notebooks his father kept while treating the King. This was the Mother Lode!

But there was a caveat. He would do this only if I received written permission from the Queen Mother.

Write to Her Majesty? That's when my American friends finally recognize my Britannic origins (I have dual UK and US citizenship). An American writer would've thought, "Who needs the Queen Mum?!?" But being born a Brit I dutifully wrote and waited. And waited. Waited some more. Snail mail crossing a continent and ocean twice can be rather slow.

The driveway to my post box was long and steep. I climbed it many times each day hoping a reply would be there.

Then one afternoon…crisp, clean, cream-colored stationery with a red coat of arms from Clarence House. Oh dear…I took a deep breath…ripped it open. Gulp, there it was, dictated by H.M. to her private secretary, saying, "Please, Mr Seidler, not during my lifetime, the memory of those events is still too painful."

Who in America waits for anything, especially an old lady. But when the Queen Mum asks an Englishman to wait…an Englishman waits. Or ends up in the Tower of London, I suppose. Besides, she was a very old lady indeed, how long would I have to wait? A year? Two or three at the most? I didn't know she'd live to be 101!

During the intervening years I obediently put the idea aside. Even with the Queen Mother's death in 2002, I didn't leap into action; other projects and obligations took priority. But in late 2005 I was diagnosed with what appeared at the time to be a particularly ominous form of cancer. Naturally I took this Christmas present rather badly, but after three or four days of feeling powerful sorry for myself, and producing a great amount of tears and mucus, I realized grief wasn't particularly good for me. It lowers one's immunity, and the immune system is your best friend.

Don't know about you, but my mind cannot walk and chew gum at the same time. I had to stop thinking about my woes, so I plunged myself into creative work. Then I thought, "Well, David, if you're not going to tell Bertie's story now, when exactly do you intend to tell it?" (Six years later I'm in remission and, to the despair of my enemies, in perfect health.)

By now I'd lost touch with Valentine Logue and assumed from his advanced age twenty-five years earlier, he was no longer with us. I had to proceed without his input or the use of those notebooks. The trouble was nobody was in the consultation room with those two men. No one kept a record of what was said. Even Logue's notebooks, when they miraculously surfaced a few weeks before filming, contained few details. I didn't want to make things up and turn it into a Hollywood fantasy. I had great reverence and affection for King George, so I approached the task with respect.

I read everything I could lay my hands on about Bertie, and a great deal has been written, so I had a mass of information concerning his life. Much less is known about Logue, but enough to glean a clear idea of his techniques. He used tongue twisters and breathing exercises, had patients intone the vowel sounds in front of an open window, had someone sit on their stomach to strengthen the diaphragm. I knew a great deal about standard techniques of the era because they had been used on me. Not exactly at the same time of course, I'm not that old, but I began speech therapy in the late 40's, which was only ten years or so later. I had marbles put in my mouth, and almost choked. I was shown that you don't stammer when you sing, nor when you cannot hear yourself. All grist for the mill.

I also knew from my own experience that mechanical techniques don't eliminate stuttering, although they're wonderful aids to fluidity of speech, once an internal change has taken place.

Over and over again Logue is referred to as being incredibly charismatic and possessing overwhelming confidence, not just in himself, but in his patients. He'd never say, "I can eliminate your stutter," but rather, "*You'll* get rid of your stutter, I'll show you things that'll help, but you'll do the real work and I know you'll succeed."

He insisted on informality and equality. He was creating friendship and trust.

Although I couldn't conclusively prove Logue read Freud, I sensed he was using the "talking cure."

Proof came in the strangest manner. I have an elderly and rather eccentric uncle, also named David, also a former stutterer, who has a small apartment in St. John's Wood, North-West London. In the early days of this project when I was doing it on my own nickel, he let me use the flat to save money. In the process he read the script and became familiar with the material. One day Uncle David said, "That chap of yours, Australian wasn't he?"

"Yes, you read correctly, the man was Australian."

"Fellow's name was Logue, wasn't it?"

"Indeed, Uncle, his name was Logue."

"Thought so. Saw the blighter for years."

"What?!?" Stunned is an understatement.

"Your grandfather, my father, wanted me to have the King's speech therapist."

"What were the sessions like?"

"Absolute rubbish. All he wanted to do was talk about Australia and his childhood and his parents and get me to talk about my parents and my childhood. Bloody waste of time."

"Uncle, you no longer stutter."

"Would've grown out of it, wouldn't I."

So there I was, correct after all. Logue used mechanical exercises combined with therapy and friendship. Since I knew the techniques, and a great deal about the King, it wasn't beyond the realm of possibility to imagine what they talked about. I entered into that task with a great sense of responsibility, hoping to get it right, or at least as close as one can, using informed imagination.

It only took me a couple of months to write a first draft. I wasn't happy with the results, so I showed it to my then wife and oft-times-but-not-always writing partner, Jacqueline Feather. She said it had "some rather nice scenes" (so diplomatic), but I was being "seduced by cinematic technique" (harrumph). She then suggested, purely as an exercise, that I write it first as a stage play. This would force me to focus on the key relationship. After all, the core of *The King's Speech* is two men in a consultation room; if I could get that tent-pole right, everything else could be hung from it like Christmas tree ornaments.

The play took a couple of months to write, and when I finished I thought, that's not half bad. I'd originally started out as a playwright, but hadn't written anything for the stage in years. So I sent *The King's Speech* out to some friends who'd managed to have real West End and Broadway careers. They raved. Trouble was, they were all ex-girl-friend actresses, and you know you can't trust them. So I sent it to an excellent playwright, Tom Minter, who is the nephew of my oldest friend. Tom had lived in London several years and had some Fringe plays produced. He was effusive and sent it to Joan Lane, ex-BBC, who helped produce special events for the Royal Family, she had even assisted with the Queen Mother's hundredth birthday party. Perfect match. This was in 2005.

Lane sent the play to Gareth Unwin and Simon Egan at Bedlam Productions. The boys of Bedlam snapped up an option and came to the brilliant conclusion it might make a screenplay.

Finally Bedlam teamed up with the UK/Australian duo of Iain Canning and Emile Sherman at See-Saw Films. They managed to scrabble together development money (as well as continuing to do a lot of heavy lifting), and I was brought over to London to transpose the play once again into a screenplay—everyone wanted to keep this very English.

That draft took less than three weeks.

From the inception I had wanted Geoffrey Rush to play Lionel Logue. I tried to approach his Australian agent and got a very cold shoulder. Then one day Joan Lane announced she had an assistant from Melbourne who was going home for the Xmas holidays and lived just a couple of blocks from Rush and would slip a synopsis through the mail slot of his front door. I was outraged at the suggestion. How…tacky. I wouldn't permit such an amateurish thing to be done in my name. Sorry, darling, gushed Lane, it's already happened.

Twenty-four hours later we got a rather subdued email from Geoffrey's Australian agent saying that Mr. Rush was interested in the material and could we send a script.

The development money hadn't developed yet, so the play version was sent. No response. Six months later I was on a trip to New Zealand to visit my son Marc and torment the trout (or perhaps it was the other way around). I was in a very remote area one could only get to by boat, it had been deluging for six straight days, and my very good tent had finally sprung leaks so my sleeping bag was sodden. I woke at 2 AM to relieve myself when I noticed my mobile phone glowing. A text message: "Rush loves TKS. Won't do play but will attach to film." The only way I could celebrate was to jump up and down on my wet sleeping bag making squelching sounds. Yipee!

We were off to the races. Having developed the project, Momentum Pictures came on board, as did Australian distributor Transmission Films. The Weinstein Company came in for the US and a number of other territories, putting up half of the budget. The finance was then completed by gap and bank financier Aegis Film Fund and a post-production deal with Molinare in the UK.

Lane had organized a one-performance staged-reading of the play at the Pleasance Theatre in Islington and invited Tom Hooper's parents. They came up to me afterwards and asked if they could send the play to their son, who was then directing the fourteen-hour miniseries *John Adams*. Why not.

There was no response for many months (fourteen hours is a lot of directing). Finally an email arrived from Tom asking if the rights were available. I replied they were not, but the job of directing was. He asked if he could see the screenplay. He was arriving the next day for the Emmy Awards.

I then did a thing which I urge my fellow writers never to emulate because it's usually a guaranteed way to end your career. I'd recently returned from London and was just finishing up the final touches of a revised draft of the script. But my producers in London hadn't seen it yet. I knew, however, if I sent it to them first, asking if they thought it was ready to show Hooper, I'd miss the boat. So I gave it to Tom first.

I delivered it at the Chateau Marmont Hotel with a big box of Allsorts to eat while he was reading. All Brits eat Allsorts while watching movies.

Tom appeared at my doorstep the next day waving the script, saying it was the best thing he'd ever been sent (maybe it was the Allsorts), and if we were filming tomorrow he'd be sleeping well tonight. I did try to remind him of that fifty-seven drafts later.

Happily the producers decided fortune favors the bold and I wasn't drummed out of the corps.

The final piece of the puzzle was Colin Firth, whose agent had heard of the project and was circling patiently. What a gift. Tom knew Firth was perfect, but to be honest I wasn't totally sure. Such a thrill, on the very first day of filming, to admit I was marvelously, stupendously wrong. Colin absolutely nailed it. He and Geoffrey deserve every award I hope they receive.

Of all the moments in the film, there is one that is especially close to my heart. It is a very crucial moment—although unfortunately earning the film a ridiculous R-rating (the same as *Chain Saw* in 3D) in the US and a 15, later reduced to 12A, in the UK. It's a scene where the King swears and says the naughty f-word (which is heard every day in every school playground everywhere). The naughty word is not in the scene to shock, nor for prurient interest. It is there because it demonstrates an important aspect of stammer therapy that I learned from my own stutter, and which all speech therapists I've ever spoken to agree has validity.

I was sixteen and my *defect* had not eased. I'd been told if a stammer doesn't disappear by the end of adolescence, the chances of its leaving decrease dramatically. That's another reason I felt Bertie was so brave; he was still slogging away through his twenties, thirties, and forties. That takes guts. Well, I got angry. My hormones were raging, but I couldn't ask a girl out. Even if she said yes, what was the point, I couldn't talk to her. Was this fair? I was a good lad who hadn't done anything dreadful to anyone. Hadn't slept with my mother or killed my father. Why was this awful burden being placed upon me? Naughty-word it! I'm a human being and I've a right to be heard. If I'm stuck with this naughty-word affliction for the rest of my life, well naughty-word it, the rest of you are just going to have to naughty-word listen to me!

That flipped an internal switch. The stutter melted away. Two weeks later I was auditioning for the school play. Even got a part. A small role in Shaw's *Androcles and the Lion*. I was a Christian, about to be eaten by a lion in the Coliseum, but I didn't stutter as I died.

I'm sure Bertie must've had a similar defiant defining moment. How else could he carry on so bravely. That's why the naughty word is there.

As for the events outside the consultations room, I tried to be as historically accurate as possible. The script was vetted by a squadron of eminent British historians who found little to change. Obviously there's some dramatic license, especially in terms of time compression; people, even kings, don't always have the good grace to live their lives in an orderly, three-act structure. But I tried as best I could to get to the truth, at least the inner truth, and so far I haven't been carted off to the Tower.

Why tell the story at all though? It's old and forgotten. Well, 1 percent of the population stammers. That's an awful lot of stuttering. A great deal of living in silence. An awful lot of emotional pain and anguish. If this film brings hope to those afflicted and understanding as to their plight, I'll be very well pleased.

The King's Speech is, however, about a great deal more than a speech impediment. It is about friendship. I'm talking about mentoring and support and a great deal of humor. We lose these deep, meaningful friendships at our peril.

Another peril is the abnegation of the social contract. With power, privilege, and wealth should come duty, service, and responsibility. When last did a CEO or bank president announce that in this vile economic climate his or her salary or bonuses were obscene, and they were donating half to charity or education or food for the poor or medical care for the needy?

Bertie understood duty. Edward the VIII did not. His was not the greatest love story ever told, it was one of the most selfish. "The woman he loved" was not only twice divorced, but a known Nazi sympathizer, and he wanted to make her Queen Wallis. He wished to be a divine right king and do whatever he damn well pleased, as opposed to doing what pleased his people and unify them for the terrible world war they were about to face. Bertie never thought he would be king—he wasn't meant to be king, wasn't trained to be king, nor with his stutter was he suited to be king. But when he had to be king, he came to the fore and did his job. Did it bloody well. No wonder he was known as Good King George. No wonder when the King died, Winston Churchill presented a funeral wreath inscribed with the phrase on the Victoria Cross: For Valour.

I trust you'll find this is still a story worth telling.

David Seidler
Santa Monica, December 2010

THE KING'S SPEECH

Written by

David Seidler

CARD:

                          1925

        King George V reigns over a quarter of the world's
                         population.

        He asks his second son, the Duke of York, to give the closing
           speech at the Empire Exhibition in Wembley, London.

1   INT. BBC BROADCASTING HOUSE, STUDIO - DAY   1

        CLOSE ON a BBC microphone of the 1920's, A formidable piece
        of machinery suspended on springs.

        A BBC NEWS READER, in a tuxedo with carnation boutonniere, is
        gargling while a TECHNICIAN holds a porcelain bowl and a
        towel at the ready. The man in the tuxedo expectorates
        discreetly into the bowl, wipes his mouth fastidiously, and
        signals to ANOTHER TECHNICIAN who produces an atomizer. The
        Reader opens his mouth, squeezes the rubber bulb, and sprays
        his inner throat. Now, he's ready.

        The reader speaks in flawless pear-shaped tones. There's no
        higher creature in the vocal world.

                          BBC NEWS READER
                    Good afternoon. This is the BBC
                    National Programme and Empire
                    Services taking you to Wembley
                    Stadium for the Closing Ceremony of
                    the Second and Final Season of the
                    Empire Exhibition.

2   INT. CORRIDOR, WEMBLEY STADIUM - DAY   2

        CLOSE ON a man's hand clutching a woman's hand.

        Woman's mouth whispers into man's ear.

                          BBC NEWS READER (V.O.)
                    58 British Colonies and Dominions
                    have taken part, making this the
                    largest Exhibition staged anywhere
                    in the world. Complete with the new
                    stadium, the Exhibition was built
                    in Wembley, Middlesex at a cost of
                    over 12 million pounds. The
                    Exhibition has attracted over 27
                    million visitors from every corner
                    of our great Empire and the rest of
                    the world.

3   INT. CONTROL ROOM, BBC BROADCASTING HOUSE - DAY   3

Technicians in suits, ties and scientific looking overcoats,
wearing bulky headphones, monitor daunting banks of valves
and dials while the Reader continues:

                    BBC NEWS READER (V.O.)
               Today the vast Stadium is filled to
               capacity with in excess of 100,000
               spectators...as regiments from His
               Majesty's Army, Navy and Air Force
               stand in review.

4   INT. GREEN ROOM - DAY   4

Nervous eyes flick towards a tunnel leading to a bright
light.

CLOSE ON - BERTIE - the Duke of York, second son of the King;
his handsome, sensitive, features look terrified.

                    BBC NEWS READER (V.O.)
               The Opening Ceremony was the first
               occasion his Majesty the King
               addressed his subjects on the
               wireless. The close of the first
               Season was the initial time His
               Royal Highness the Prince of Wales
               had broadcast. And today His Royal
               Highness the Duke of York will give
               his inaugural broadcast to the
               Nation and the World.

WIDEN TO REVEAL his young wife, truly an English rose.

                    ELIZABETH
               Time to go.

He stares straight ahead, frozen. She gives him a loving
peck on the cheek, quickly rubbing off a fleck of lipstick.

                    BBC NEWS READER (V.O.)
               Leading us in prayer will be the
               Right Honourable and Most Reverend
               Archbishop of York, Primate of all
               England and Metropolitan. Now we go
               live to Wembley Stadium, where His
               Royal Highness the Duke of York
               will read his message from the
               King.

COSMO LANG - comes up to Bertie. Tries to be helpful but
makes him more nervous.

>   COSMO LANG
> I am sure you will be splendid.
> Just take your time.

The last bars of "God Save The King" echo down the corridor.

ROBERT WOOD, the Chief BBC Engineer on Location whispers:

>   WOOD
> Let the microphone do the work,
> sir.

Wood checks his watch.

>   WOOD (CONT'D)
> Thirty seconds, sir.

Bertie braces his shoulders manfully, but without an ounce of confidence, closes his eyes, nods, opens them, and reluctantly goes through the tunnel towards the light, like a prize-fighter entering the arena, to be greeted by the roar of the crowd.

5   EXT.   ROYAL PODIUM - DAY   5

HAND-HELD CAMERA, BERTIE'S POV: far ahead, at a seemingly impossible distance, is the huge intimidating microphone, the only thing between the terrified observer and 100,000 people.

Silence falls over the stadium.

Overhead, thick roiling clouds.

BERTIE approaches...like a death march.

Bertie's eyes widen in terror as he reaches the microphone. The red transmission light blinks four times then glows solid red. Bertie is live.

6   INT. CONTROL ROOM, BBC BROADCASTING HOUSE - DAY   6

Technicians stare at dials and listen to the hiss of silence.

The Reader and Floor Manager glance at each other nervously.

7   EXT.   SPECTATOR STAND, EMPIRE STADIUM -DAY   7

In the tense silence PAN THROUGH some of the crowd waiting with growing discomfort. In particular we notice a father and son watching intently.

8   EXT.   ROYAL PODIUM - DAY   8

          Bertie is frozen at the microphone. His neck and jaw muscles
          contract and quiver.

                              BERTIE
                    I have received from his Majesty
                    the K-K-K

          [For ease of reading, Bertie's stammer will not be indicated
          from this point in the script.]

          The stammer careens back at him, amplified and distorted by
          the stadium PA system.

          CU huge metal speakers.

          CU soldiers at rigid attention.

          CU Wood, he shuts his eyes.

          CU Cosmo Lang, expressionless.

          CU Elizabeth, dying.

          Bertie gulps for air like a beached fish and attempts to
          continue:

                              BERTIE (CONT'D)
                    ...the King, the following gracious
                    message...

          He can't get the word out. SPLAT...the first drops of rain
          begin to fall.

9   EXT. 145 PICADILLY - NEW DAY   9

          Establishing shot of an imposing Georgian edifice, opposite
          Hyde Park Corner. In the foreground people pay their respects
          at the WWI monument with fresh wreaths.

          A Rover sedan - definitive doctor's car of the era - arrives.
          A FOOTMAN scurries down the steps to meet it as the STEWARD
          opens the front door.

10   INT. DRAWING ROOM, 145 PICCADILLY - CONTINUOUS   10

          CLOSE ON SIR BLANDINE-BENTHAM - an elderly, unctuous,
          studiedly-distinguished physician who simultaneously manages
          to combine pontificating and obsequiousness.

> SIR BLANDINE-BENTHAM
> Inhale deep into your lungs.
> Relaxes your larynx, does it not?

Bertie is seated nervously on the edge of a couch, gripping a cigarette between thumb and forefinger, placed in the middle of his mouth.

Elizabeth watches from across the room.

> SIR BLANDINE-BENTHAM (CONT'D)
> Cigarette smoking calms the nerves
> and gives you confidence.

Bertie clearly feels nothing of the sort. Smiling ingratiatingly, the doctor produces a medical cannister from his bag.

> SIR BLANDINE-BENTHAM (CONT'D)
> If Your Highness will be so kind as
> to open his hand...

Bertie unclenches a fist.

> SIR BLANDINE-BENTHAM (CONT'D)
> Thank you so very much.

Opening the container, with forceps he removes five marbles from an antiseptic solution and places them onto Bertie's palm.

> SIR BLANDINE-BENTHAM (CONT'D)
> Sterilized. Now...if I may take the
> liberty?...insert them into your
> mouth.

Bertie obeys, mortified. The doctor hands Bertie a book from his bag.

> SIR BLANDINE-BENTHAM (CONT'D)
> Would you be so kind as to read.

Bertie blanches, his neck muscles twitch and constrict

> BERTIE
> I...

He can't even say "can't".

> SIR BLANDINE-BENTHAM
> Just take your time. Relax.

Bertie is unable to do it. Elizabeth watches with growing discomfort.

> ELIZABETH
> Excuse me, Doctor. What is the
> purpose of this?

> SIR BLANDINE-BENTHAM
> The classic approach that cured
> Demosthenes.

> ELIZABETH
> That was in Ancient Greece. Has it
> worked since?

Blandine-Bentham passes Bertie a book.

> SIR BLANDINE-BENTHAM
> Now if you would be so kind as to
> read. A wealth of words.

Bertie tries. It is excruciating.

> SIR BLANDINE-BENTHAM (CONT'D)
> Fight against those marbles Your
> Royal Highness. Enunciate!

As Bertie struggles.

> SIR BLANDINE-BENTHAM (CONT'D)
> A little more concentration your
> Royal Higness.

Bertie spits the marbles out.

> BERTIE
> (explodes)
> I nearly swallowed the damned
> things!

Bertie storms out as Elizabeth tries to placate the doctor.

> ELIZABETH
> Thank you so much, Doctor, it's
> been most interesting.

Elizabeth goes through to the adjoining room to find Bertie.

11   INT. BERTIE'S STUDY, 145 PICCADILLY - CONTINUOUS   11

Bertie is struggling to light a cigarette.

> ELIZABETH
> Temper, Bertie darling, temper.
> Tick, tock, tick, tock.

> BERTIE
> Insert marbles! He can insert his
> own bloody marbles....!

[Note: when he speaks with his wife there's hardly any
hesitation]

Elizabeth smiles as she lights the cigarette for him.

> ELIZABETH
> You can't keep doing this, Bertie.

> BERTIE
> I know. Promise me: *no more*.

                                              CUT TO:

12   EXT. HARLEY STREET - NEW DAY   12

A thick grey wet blanket...

Out of which materializes the moisture splattered hood of a
large AUSTIN.

Elizabeth, inside, determinedly glances out.

The vehicle noses thru a pea-soup fog. The York's HOUSE
DETECTIVE is walking a few feet in front of the car, finding
the way.

After a moment, the House Detective signals the driver to
stop. Elizabeth peers out the window.

POV - in the gloom the least attractive and most ill-
maintained of the Georgian terraced houses.

Elizabeth looks disappointed and dubious. She gets out of the
car. Instructing the House Detective to wait outside, she
enters the building.

13   INT. GROUND FLOOR ENTRANCE, HARLEY STREET - CONTINUOUS   13

Elizabeth enters, somewhat dampened, the white silk roses
decorating her hat now limp.

There is a cramped elevator which is whirring noisily and a
winding staircase.

Elizabeth is even more dubious.

14   INT. ELEVATOR - CONTINUOUS   14

        Elizabeth inside the cramped elevator.

        She surveys the buttons. The bottom one reads "Basement: L.
        Logue, Speech Defects".

        She closes the inner gate of the elevator and presses the
        bottom button.

        Nothing.

        Confused, she opens the inner gate, closes the outer gate
        then the inner gate and presses the button again. The
        elevator jumps downwards.

15   INT. WAITING ROOM, LOGUE'S CHAMBERS - CONTINUOUS   15

        Umbrella stand, coat rack, wooden waiting bench: that's all.

        She looks about. The area is devoid of life. Coughs. No
        response. Calls imperiously:

                        ELIZABETH
                Hello. Is anyone there?

        From behind a door:

                        MUFFLED VOICE (O.S.)
                I'm just in the loo.

        Princess Elizabeth is not used to this sort of thing. She's
        further appalled by the loud gurgling of a toilet being
        flushed, and startled by the entrance of - LIONEL LOGUE - a
        tall, middle-aged man with strong features. His demeanor is
        friendly, yet professional.

                        LIONEL
                "Poor and content is rich and rich
                enough"

                        ELIZABETH
                I beg your pardon?

                        LIONEL
                Shakespeare. I'm sorry, there's no
                receptionist. I like to keep things
                simple. How are you Mrs Johnson?
                I'm afraid you're late.

        Offers his hand. She takes it, a little gingerly.

                    ELIZABETH
I'm afraid I am.

                    LIONEL
Where's Mr Johnson?

                    ELIZABETH
He doesn't know I'm here.

                    LIONEL
That's not a promising start.

                    ELIZABETH
My husband has seen everyone to no
avail. He's given up hope.

                    LIONEL
He hasn't seen me.

                    ELIZABETH
You're awfully sure of yourself.

                    LIONEL
I'm sure of anyone who wants to be
cured.

                    ELIZABETH
Naturally he wishes to be cured. My
husband is required to speak
publicly.

                    LIONEL
Perhaps he should change jobs.

                    ELIZABETH
He can't.

                    LIONEL
Indentured servitude?

                    ELIZABETH
Something of that nature.

                    LIONEL
Well have your hubby pop
by...Tuesday would be good...to
give his personal history and I'll
make a frank appraisal.

                    ELIZABETH
I do *not* have a "*hubby*". We don't
'pop'. We *never* talk about our
private lives. You must come to us.

LIONEL
Sorry, Mrs J, my game, my turf, my rules.

ELIZABETH
And what if my husband were the Duke of York?

LIONEL
The Duke of York?

ELIZABETH
Yes the Duke of York.

LIONEL
I thought the appointment was for "Johnson"? Forgive me, your Royal...?

ELIZABETH
Highness.

LIONEL
Your Royal Highness.

ELIZABETH
Johnson was used during the Great War when the Navy didn't want the enemy to know 'he' was aboard. We are operating under the strictest of confidences.

LIONEL
Of course. I'm considered the enemy?

ELIZABETH
You will be if you remain un-obliging.

LIONEL
How did you find me?

ELIZABETH
The President of the Speech Therapists Society.

LIONEL
Eileen McCleod? She's a sport.

ELIZABETH
Dr McCleod warned me your antipodean methods were "unorthodox and controversial".
                    (MORE)

                    ELIZABETH (CONT'D)
          I warned her...they were not my
          favorite words.

                    LIONEL
          I succeed.

                    ELIZABETH
          So she says.

                    LIONEL
          I can cure your husband. But for my
          method to work there must be trust
          and total equality in the safety of
          my consultation room. No
          exceptions.

                    ELIZABETH
          Well then, in that case...

Pause.

                    ELIZABETH (CONT'D)
          When can you start?

16   EXT. SOUTH KENSINGTON STREET - LATE AFTERNOON   16

A well-used Morris Oxford pulls up, driven by Lionel's eldest
son - LAURIE. Lionel is the passenger. As he gets out:

                    LIONEL
          Still sounds a bit rough.

                    LAURIE
          You make me drive too slowly, Dad!

                    LIONEL
          Did you pick mum up from Bridge?

                    LAURIE
          Yes, I've hardly been out of the
          car all day.

They enter a modest dwelling.

17   INT. DINING AREA OF LIVING-ROOM, LOGUE FLAT - EVENING   17

Lionel and MYRTLE are finishing up at the table with their
three sons. As well as Laurie and ANTONY, there's their
studious middle son VALENTINE, 17, his nose buried in a stack
of science books.

Lionel is bursting to tell Myrtle something.

                    LIONEL
          I had a special visitor today.

                    ANTONY
          May I be excused?

                    MYRTLE
               (to Lionel)
          Oh yes?

                    LIONEL
          You must stay, bored stupid,
          listening to your parents' inane
          conversation.

                    ANTONY
               (grinning)
          Thanks, dad!

                    LIONEL
          And mum.

                    ANTONY
          And mum!

                    MYRTLE
          How special is special?

                    LAURIE
          Me too?

                    LIONEL
          A girl?

                    LAURIE
          What else?

He and Antony start to leave.

                    MYRTLE
          Take your plates.

                    LIONEL
          Special to the point of someone I
          can't really talk about.

The boys grabs their plates and exit. Lionel looks at
Valentine, nose still buried in his text.

                    LIONEL (CONT'D)
          Doctor? Doctor? You can go as well.

                         VALENTINE
                     (still studying)
             I'm fine.

Lionel clears Valentine's plate. Valentine goes back to his
book and scientific oblivion.

                         MYRTLE
             Not too high and mighty I hope?

                         LIONEL
             Aah.

Antony burst back in, model airplane in hand, doing barrel
rolls with sound effects, bombing Valentine with a tea towel.

                         MYRTLE
             Not someone who'd...call attention?
             Why bring it up if you can't talk
             about it?

Silence.

                         LIONEL
             Myrtle, just a woman looking to
             help her husband.

They realize from engine noises that Antony is under the
table.

                         LIONEL (CONT'D)
                     (trying to make light of
                      it, not quite succeeding)
             And I had a 'call'.

                         MYRTLE
             Oh yes.

Valentine looks up from his book.

                         VALENTINE
             What's the Illiotibial Tract, Dad?

                         LIONEL
             If you don't know, look it up.

                         VALENTINE
             Right.

Starts turning pages.

                         LIONEL
             Could be fun.

> MYRTLE
> It always is.

> LIONEL
> They're a highly regarded group.
> From Putney.

> MYRTLE
> I'm sure you'll be splendid.

18   EXT. YORK HOUSE, 145 PICADILLY - NIGHT   18

Lights are on in the upper windows. A double-decker bus
passes on the wet street.

> ELIZABETH (V.O.)
> Tomorrow, Chapter IV.

19   INT. CORRIDOR, 145 PICCADILLY - CONTINUOUS   19

PAN OVER THE BACKS of 36 impeccably groomed horses. It takes
a moment to realize they are toy horses, lined up with
precision.

> ELIZABETH (V.O.)
> 'The Flight'.

> BERTIE (V.O.)
> Oh, to fly away!

20   INT. CHILDREN'S NURSERY, YORK HOUSE - CONTINUOUS   20

Elizabeth, fashionably attired for an evening-out, is curled
on a bearskin rug reading to a little girl - LILIBET, 10 -
who claps her hands primly, and her younger sister - MARGARET
ROSE, 5.

As Elizabeth closes the book ("Peter Pan"), Bertie, handsome
in a tuxedo, comments:

> BERTIE
> Weren't they lucky!

Within his family Bertie's stammer is virtually absent.

> MARGARET ROSE
> Now Papa tell a story!

> BERTIE
> Could I be a penguin instead?

He drops to his knees and waddles. In his tux he looks like a penguin. Margaret Rose giggles, but is undeterred.

>   MARGARET ROSE
> Tell me a penguin story, please.

Called upon to perform, the stammer returns slightly, but the girls listen raptly, ignoring their father's minor impediment, and it fades.

>   BERTIE
> There were once two princesses
> whose Papa had been turned into a
> penguin by the local witch. This
> was inconvenient because he loved
> to hold his princesses in his arms
> and you can't do that if you're a
> penguin, you have wings like
> herrings.

>   MARGARET ROSE
> Herrings don't have wings.

>   BERTIE
> His wings were the shape of
> herrings. To make matters worse she
> sent him to the South Pole which is
> an awfully long walk if you can't
> fly.

>   LILIBET
> You can't walk from the South Pole!

>   ELIZABETH
> Shh!

>   BERTIE
> Exactly. When he reached the water
> and dived in he found he *could* fly.
> Fly through the depths. So fast, in
> fact, that he was in Southampton
> Waters by lunchtime. From there he
> caught the 2.30 to Weybridge,
> changed at Clapham Junction and
> asked a passing Mallard the way to
> Buckingham Palace. He swam up the
> Thames and came out of a plughole,
> giving Mama, the cook and Mrs
> Whittaker quite a shock. The
> princesses heard the commotion and
> hurried to the kitchen where they
> gave the penguin a good scrub, a
> mackerel and a kiss.
>   (MORE)

                    BERTIE (CONT'D)
          And as they kissed him guess what
          he turned into?

                    LILIBET AND MARGARET ROSE
          A handsome prince!

                    BERTIE
          A short-tailed Albatross. With
          wings big enough to wrap around
          both his precious girls together.
                    (He hugs them both
                     together)

                    ELIZABETH
          Now time for bed.

                    BERTIE
          Take the saddles of your horsies,
          brush them, feed them and to bed.

21   INT. STAIRCASE - CONTINUOUS   21

       As they leave for the night:

                    ELIZABETH
          Will she be there?

                    BERTIE
          My brother's insisting.

                    ELIZABETH
          Is he serious?

                    BERTIE
          About our coming to dinner?

                    ELIZABETH
          No. About her!

                    BERTIE
          A married American? He can't be.

                    ELIZABETH
          She can. By the way I think I found
          someone rather interesting. On
          Harley Street. A doctor.

                    BERTIE
          Out of the question. I'm not having
          this conversation again. The
          matter's settled.

                        ELIZABETH
            His approach seems rather
            different....

22   INT. A STAGE - DAY   22

In a church or school hall, out of hours.

                        MUFFLED VOICE (O.S.)
            Now?

From the auditorium:

                        DIRECTOR (O.C.)
            Now!

Lionel comes onstage.

                        LIONEL
            "Now..."
                (begins again)
            "Now is the winter of our
            discontent
            Made glorious summer by this sun of
            York."

His elocution is flawless. The acting is unconvincing.

                        LIONEL (CONT'D)
            "And all the clouds that lour'd
            upon our house
            In the deep bosom of the ocean
            buried.
            Now are our brows bound with
            victorious wreaths;
            Our bruised arms hung up for
            monuments..."

                        DIRECTOR
            Thank you.

Lionel peers into the darkness, his eyes hoping.

                        DIRECTOR (CONT'D)
            Lovely diction, Mr...

                        LIONEL
            Logue. Lionel Logue.

                        DIRECTOR
            Well, Lionel, I didn't hear the
            cries of a deformed creature
            yearning to be King.
                (MORE)

                 DIRECTOR (CONT'D)
Nor did I realize Richard the Third
was King of the Colonies.

                 LIONEL
I know the lines. I've played the
role before.

                 DIRECTOR
Sydney?

                 LIONEL
Perth.

                 DIRECTOR
Major theater town, is it?

                 LIONEL
Enthusiastic.

                 DIRECTOR
Ah.

                 LIONEL
I was well reviewed.

                 DIRECTOR
Yes...well...Lionel, I think our
dramatic society is looking for
someone slightly younger and a
little more regal.

23   INT. GROUND FLOOR ENTRANCE, 146 HARLEY STREET   23

The Yorks enter the tiny elevator.

Bertie shuts the inner gate.

                 ELIZABETH
             (indicating outer gate)
No, darling, shut that one first.

Bertie gets the gates closed and Elizabeth presses the
button.

                 BERTIE
How did you find this...physician?

                 ELIZABETH
             (poker-faced)
Classifieds, next to "French model,
Shepherd's Market".

Bertie tries to smile despite his mood, but doesn't make a
job of it.

>   ELIZABETH (CONT'D)
>   He comes highly recommended.
>   Charges substantial fees in order
>   to help the poor. (realizes) Oh
>   dear, perhaps he's a Bolshevik?!

24   INT. LOGUE'S WAITING ROOM - DAY   24

Bertie and Elizabeth enter. She explains in a whisper:

>   ELIZABETH
>   No receptionist. He likes to keep
>   things simple.

Elizabeth glances nervously at the lavatory door.

>   ELIZABETH (CONT'D)
>   (loudly)
>   The Johnsons.

From the inner office.

>   LIONEL (O.S.)
>   Finishing up.

Elizabeth is relieved the voice isn't coming from the lav.

The consultation room door opens and a young boy - WILLY -
comes out.

>   WILLY
>   You can go in now, "Mr. Johnson".
>   (then to Elizabeth)
>   Dr Logue says...

>   LIONEL (O.S.)
>   Lionel!

>   WILLY
>   Lionel says...wait here if you
>   wish, Mrs Johnson. Or, it being a p-
>   pleasant day, p-perhaps take a
>   stroll.
>   (to the consultation room)
>   Was that alright...Lionel?

Lionel appears at the door.

>   LIONEL
>   Bloody marvellous. You can stay
>   here and wait for your mum. Mr.
>   Johnson, do come in.

Lionel nods at "Mrs Johnson".

The Yorks look at each other. Elizabeth takes a seat.

25   INT. LOGUE'S CONSULTATION ROOM - DAY   25

A different universe from the Spartan waiting area. A world
of books - piles of them spilling everywhere. Two slightly
shabby, but comfortable armchairs. Well-worn Turkish rug.
Hotplate and two chipped mugs. Recording apparatus. Model
airplanes.

>   LIONEL
>   He's a good lad, Willy. He could
>   hardly make a sound, you know, when
>   he first came to me.

Lionel catches Bertie staring at the airplanes.

>   LIONEL (CONT'D)
>   My boys made those. Good, aren't
>   they. Please, make yourself
>   comfortable.

Bertie sits uneasily on an armchair. Lionel goes to sit at a
distance.

>   LIONEL (CONT'D)
>   I was told not not to sit too
>   close.

Bertie remains silent.

>   LIONEL (CONT'D)
>   I was also told, speaking with a
>   Royal, one waits for the Royal to
>   choose the topic.

>   BERTIE
>   Waiting for me to commence a
>   conversation one can wait a rather
>   long wait.

[Although Bertie's stammer in the consultation room will
fade, it is a gradual process.]

Silence.

                    LIONEL
          Know any jokes?

                    BERTIE
          Timing isn't my strong suit.

Silence. They stare at each other.

                    LIONEL
          Cuppa tea?

                    BERTIE
          No thank you.

                    LIONEL
          I think I'll have one.

Turns on the hot plate.

                    BERTIE
          Aren't you going to start treating
          me Dr Logue?

                    LIONEL
          Only if you're interested in being
          treated. Please, call me Lionel.

                    BERTIE
          I prefer Doctor.

                    LIONEL
          I prefer Lionel. What'll I call
          you?

                    BERTIE
          Your Royal Highness, then Sir after
          that.

                    LIONEL
          A bit formal for here. What about
          your name?

                    BERTIE
          Prince Albert Frederick Arthur
          George?

                    LIONEL
          How about Bertie?

                    BERTIE
             (flushes)
          Only my family uses that.

LIONEL
Perfect. In here, it's better if
we're equals.

BERTIE
If we were equal I wouldn't be
here. I'd be at home with my wife
and no-one would give a damn.

Bertie starts to light a cigarette from a silver case.

LIONEL
Don't do that.

Bertie gives him an astonished look.

BERTIE
I'm sorry?

LIONEL
Sucking smoke into your lungs will
kill you.

BERTIE
My physicians say it relaxes the
throat.

LIONEL
They're idiots.

BERTIE
They've all been knighted.

LIONEL
Makes it official then. My
'castle', my rules. What was your
earliest memory?

BERTIE
What an earth do you mean?

LIONEL
First recollection.

BERTIE
        (stammer growing in
         intensity)
I'm not here to discuss personal
matters.

LIONEL
Why're you here then?

                    BERTIE
            (exploding - stammer free)
        Because I bloody well stammer!

                    LIONEL
        Temper.

                    BERTIE
        One of my many faults.

                    LIONEL
        When did the defect start?

                    BERTIE
        I've always been this way!

                    LIONEL
            (quietly)
        I doubt that.

                    BERTIE
        Don't tell me! It's *my* defect!

                    LIONEL
            (calmly)
        It's my field. I assure you, no
        infant starts to speak with a
        stammer. When did it start?

                    BERTIE
            (annoyed)
        Four or five.

                    LIONEL
        That's typical.

                    BERTIE
        So I've been told.
            (quickly adds)
        I can't remember not doing it.

                    LIONEL
        That I believe. Do you hesitate
        when you think?

                    BERTIE
        Don't be ridiculous.

                    LIONEL
        One of *my* many faults. How about
        when you talk to yourself?

Bertie is silent.

                    LIONEL (CONT'D)
          Everyone natters occasionally,
          Bertie.

                    BERTIE
          Stop calling me that!

                    LIONEL
          I'm not going to call you anything
          else.

                    BERTIE
          Then we shan't speak!

Silence. The kettle whistles. Lionel makes himself a cup of
tea.

                    BERTIE (CONT'D)
          Are you charging for this, Doctor?

                    LIONEL
          A fortune. So, Bertie...when you
          talk to yourself, do you stammer?

                    BERTIE
          Of course not!

                    LIONEL
          Thus proving your impediment isn't
          a permanent part of you. What do
          you think was the cause?

                    BERTIE
          I don't know! I don't care! I
          stammer. And no one can fix it.

                    LIONEL
          Bet you, Bertie, you can read
          flawlessly, right here, right now.

Bertie snorts dismissively.

                    LIONEL (CONT'D)
          And if I win, I get to ask
          questions.

                    BERTIE
          And if I win?

                    LIONEL
          You don't have to answer.

                    BERTIE
          One usually wagers money.

> LIONEL
> A bob each to sweeten it? See your
> shilling.

> BERTIE
> I don't carry cash.

> LIONEL
> I had a funny feeling you mightn't.

Logue fishes two coins from his pocket and puts them on the
table.

> LIONEL (CONT'D)
> Stake you. Pay me back next time.

> BERTIE
> If there is a next time.

> LIONEL
> (nods)
> I haven't agreed to take you on.

Logue has uncovered a piece of apparatus, a recording device
with earphones. He sets a blank disc onto the turntable and
positions a microphone, then hands Bertie an open book.
Bertie glares at it defiantly.

> BERTIE
> I can't possibly read this.

> LIONEL
> Then you owe me a shilling for not
> trying.

Furious, Bertie opens the book and reads, stammers badly and
gets worse.

> BERTIE
> "To be or not to be, That is the
> question. Whether it is wiser..."
> There!

He hands the book back to Lionel.

> BERTIE (CONT'D)
> I can't read!

> LIONEL
> I haven't finished yet.

Lionel returns the book to Bertie and turns to some recording
apparatus on a nearby table.

> LIONEL (CONT'D)
> I'm going to record your voice and
> then play it back to you on the
> same machine. This is brilliant.
> It's the latest thing from America:
> a Silvertone.

He hands Bertie a pair of heavily padded earphones. Bertie
doesn't want to take them.

> LIONEL (CONT'D)
> There's a bob in this, mate. You
> can go home rich!

Bertie reluctantly puts them on. Logue turns a dial. LOUD
MUSIC is heard. Bertie takes off the earphones. The music
stops.

> BERTIE
> You're playing music.

> LIONEL
> I know.

> BERTIE
> How can I hear what I'm saying?!

> LIONEL
> Surely a Prince's brain knows what
> its mouth is doing?

> BERTIE
> You're not well acquainted with
> Royal Princes, are you?

Bertie replaces the earphones. Again, the LOUD MUSIC. His
mouth moves as he reads, but all that can be heard is the
music. Finished, Bertie takes off the earphones and the music
ceases. Bertie reaches for the coins, but Logue snatches
them.

> BERTIE (CONT'D)
> Hopeless. Hopeless!

> LIONEL
> You were sublime. Would I lie to a
> prince of the realm to win twelve-
> pence?

> BERTIE
> I've no idea what an Australian
> might do for that sort of money.

                    LIONEL
          Shall I play it?

                    BERTIE
          No.

                    LIONEL
          If you prefer, we'll just get on to
          the questions.

                    BERTIE
          Thank you Doctor, I don't feel this
          is for me.

He heads for the door. Logue puts the record in a brown paper
dust jacket and hands it to Bertie.

                    LIONEL
          Sir? The recording is free. Please
          keep it as a souvenir?

Lionel opens the door for Bertie and closes it behind him

26   INT. LOGUE'S WAITING ROOM - DAY   26

Elizabeth looks up at Bertie hopefully.

                    BERTIE
          No

Elizabeth nods and rises. They walk towards the door
together.

                    ELIZABETH
          Ah well.

27   EXT. SANDRINGHAM ESTATE - DAY   27

Establishing shot in the snow.

A cold and commanding voice is heard:

                    KING GEORGE V (O.S.)
          *For the present, the work to which
          we are all equally bound, is to
          arrive at a reasoned
          tranquillity...*

28   INT. THE KING'S STUDY, SANDRINGHAM ESTATE - CONTINUOUS   28

The King's study, which resembles an orderly naval captain's cabin, except for a desk littered with stamp albums, has been converted into an ad hoc broadcasting studio. KING GEORGE V is a barrel-chested man with Naval beard and uniform.

He is giving his Christmas address via the radio.

>   KING GEORGE V (CONT'D)
> *...within our borders, to regain*
> *prosperity in this time of*
> *depression without self-seeking and*
> *to carry with us those whom the*
> *burden of past years has*
> *disheartened or overborne. To all,*
> *to each, I wish a Happy Christmas.*
> *God bless you.*

The red light next to him goes out, indicating the broadcast is complete. Robert Wood, the BBC technician from Wembley, stands by as well as an official photographer.

King George V looks at Bertie, who is standing next to him.

>   KING GEORGE V (CONT'D)
> Easy when you know how.

>   PHOTOGRAPHER
> Sir?

Bertie moves away and the photographer captures the King, seated at his desk.

>   KING GEORGE V
>   (to Bertie)
> Have a go yourself.

>   WOOD
> Congratulations, Sir.

>   KING GEORGE V
> Ah, Mr Wood. Splendid fellow. Chap
> taught me everything I know: let
> the microphone do the work.

>   WOOD
> Sir.

>   KING GEORGE V
> Thank you.

Wood and the photographer take that as their cue to leave.

                    KING GEORGE V (CONT'D)
Sit up, straight back, face boldly
up to the bloody thing and stare it
square in the eye, as you would any
decent Englishman. Show who's in
command.

Bertie regards the BBC microphone as though it were an alien
creature.

                    BERTIE
D-d-don't thu-thu-think I c-c-can.

In the presence of his father, Bertie's stammering returns in
full form, his breathing short and shallow, the neck muscles
in spasms.

                    KING GEORGE V
This devilish device will change
everything if you won't. In the
past all a King had to do was look
respectable in uniform and not fall
off his horse. Now we must invade
people's homes and ingratiate
ourselves with them. This family is
reduced to those lowest, basest of
all creatures...we've
become...actors!

                    BERTIE
Papa, we're not a family, we're a
firm.

His father shoots Bertie a surprised look: does the lad have
a brain after all?

                    KING GEORGE V
The most successful institution in
history. Our cousins wear crowns
throughout Europe. A dozen of them!
Sitting on thrones is our business!
Yet any moment some of us may be
out of work. Your darling
brother... The only wife he appears
interested in is invariably the
wife of another!

                    BERTIE
        (tries to brighten things)
He's broken off with Lady Furness.

                    KING GEORGE V
And taken up a *Mrs* Simpson, a woman
with two husbands living!
        (MORE)

                    KING GEORGE V (CONT'D)
          Had the audacity to present her to
          me at Georgie's wedding. I told him
          straight no divorced person could
          ever be received at court. He said
          she made him sublimely happy. I
          imagined that was because she was
          sleeping with him. "I give you my
          word we've never had immoral
          relations," he replied. Stared
          square into his father's eyes...
          and lied.

Bertie groans.

                    KING GEORGE V (CONT'D)
          When I'm dead that boy will ruin
          himself, this family, and this
          nation, within twelve months.
          Who'll pick up the pieces? Herr
          Hitler, intimidating half of
          Europe, Marshall Stalin the other
          half? Who'll stand between us, the
          jackboots, and the proletarian
          abyss? You? With your older brother
          shirking his duties, you're going
          to have to do a lot more of this.
                    (nodding towards the
                     microphone)
          Have a go yourself.

Bertie tries to read the King's speech.

                    BERTIE
          Through one of the m-

                    KING GEORGE V
          Get it out boy!

                    BERTIE
          ...m-marvels of m-

                    KING GEORGE V
          Modern - just take your time - form
          your words carefully

                    BERTIE
          Science, I am enabled, this C-

                    KING GEORGE V
          Relax!
                    (off Bertie's continued
                     inability)
          Just try it!

                              BERTIE
                    ...this Christmas Day, to speak to
                    all my p-

                              KING GEORGE V
                              (all patience lost)
                    Do it!

29   INT. BERTIE'S STUDY, YORK HOUSE - NEW NIGHT   29

Bertie lies on a chaise longue, smoking.

                              BERTIE
                              (to himself)
                    Lying bastard.

Bertie gets up and retrieves the recording he made with
Lionel. He walks to a Victoria stand, lifts the arm, places
the steel needle. It slips and slides across the records
surface, as steel needles do. But what he hears is poetic and
flowing:

                    BERTIE'S RECORDED VOICE
                    "To be, or not to be, - that is the
                    question: -

Elizabeth enters, unseen by Bertie and listens.

                    BERTIE'S RECORDED VOICE (CONT'D)
                    "...whether tis nobler in the mind
                    to suffer The slings and arrows of
                    outrageous fortune,
                    Or to take arms against a sea of
                    troubles, And by opposing end
                    them.."

Hold on Elizabeth, stunned: Unable to hear himself, her
husband speaks perfectly for the very first time.

30   INT. LOGUE'S CONSULTATION ROOM - NEW DAY   30

Bertie and Elizabeth have returned to the consultation room.

                              BERTIE
                    Strictly business. No personal
                    nonsense.

                              ELIZABETH
                    I thought I'd made that very clear
                    in our interview.

Logue is silent, then:

                    LIONEL
Got the shilling you owe me?

                    BERTIE
No I don't!

                    LIONEL
Didn't think so.

                    BERTIE
Besides, you tricked me!

                    LIONEL
No, I showed you what you can do.
          (tries to get them to
          understand)
What you're asking will only deal
with the surface of the problem.

                    ELIZABETH
That's sufficient. My husband has
difficulties with his speech. Just
deal with that.

                    BERTIE
I'm willing to work hard, Doctor
Logue...

                    LIONEL
Lionel.

                    BERTIE
Are you willing to do your part?

Logue considers, then tells Bertie:

                    LIONEL
Alright. You want mechanics? We
need to relax your throat muscles
and strengthen your tongue. By
repeating tongue twisters for
example. "I am a thistle-sifter. I
have a sieve of sifted thistles and
a sieve of unsifted thistles.
Because I am a thistle sifter."

                    BERTIE
Fine.

                    LIONEL
You have a flabby tummy, we must
build up the strength in your
diaphragm. Simple mechanics.

                    ELIZABETH
          That is all we ask.

                    LIONEL
          And that's about a shilling's
          worth.

                    BERTIE
          Forget about the blessed shilling!
               (calm again)
          Perhaps, upon occasion, I shall
          request some assistance in coping
          with a minor event. Will that be
          agreeable?

                    LIONEL
          Of course.

                    ELIZABETH
          That will be the full extent of
          your services.

                    BERTIE
          Shall I see you next week?

                    LIONEL
          I shall see you every day.

On Bertie, reacting.

MONTAGE

Many different sessions, many different days, all in the
consultation room.

CU of Bertie's mouth. Humming.

                    LIONEL (CONT'D)
          Hum for as long as you like.
          Hmmmmmmmmmmm. And when you're ready,
          "Mother".

                    BERTIE
          Hmmmmmmmmmmmmmmmother.

                    LIONEL
          Beaut.

                                              CUT TO:

                    LIONEL (CONT'D)
          A simple outward breath. "FFFFF"
          Wait for the "aa". "FFFFFather".
          Just slide into it.

                         BERTIE
                FFFFFFFFFFFather.

                                              CUT TO:

                         LIONEL
                Feel the loosening of the jaw

Bertie and Lionel both have their individual hands clasped
and are shaking them, vibrating their chest and loosening
their jaw. As their jaws wobble, they omit a vibrating sound.

                         BERTIE
                Ahahahahhahahahahahahahahahahahah.

                         LIONEL
                    (at the same time)
                Ahahahahahahahahahahahahahahahaha,

                                              CUT TO:

Bertie lies on the floor

                         LIONEL (CONT'D)
                Deep breath. Expand your
                chest...lift your diaphragm...allow
                the column of air into your
                stomach...How do you feel?

                         BERTIE
                Full of hot air.

                         LIONEL
                Isn't that what public speaking is
                all about?

Bertie inhales deeply.

                                              CUT TO:

Some fast cuts. Lionel handing him a cup of tea. Bertie doing
slow breathing exercises. Bertie shouting something in
frustration.

                         BERTIE
                I will never get that.

                         LIONEL
                Yes you can, come on, come on.

                                              CUT TO:

Bertie's on the floor again.

                    LIONEL (CONT'D)
          Deep breath. Hold.

He turns to Elizabeth.

                    LIONEL (CONT'D)
          Now Ma'am, while you are here, you
          could again be of great assistance.
          If you'd kindly sit on your
          husband's stomach.

                    ELIZABETH
          Oh yes?

                    LIONEL
          Gently of course.

Elizabeth sits gingerly on Bertie's stomach, asking
solicitously:

                    ELIZABETH
          Are you alright, Bertie?

Bertie nods.

                    LIONEL
          Now exhale slowly...can you feel
          that resistance, Bertie? Down goes
          your Royal Highness...inhale
          slowly...and...up comes your Royal
          Highness. Exhale and down. Yes.
          Inhale and up. You get the idea.

                    ELIZABETH
          This is actually quite good fun,
          Bertie.

                    LIONEL
          Do it at home. Doesn't have to be
          you, of course, but I thought he'd
          prefer you to one of the staff.

Lionel encourages Bertie to move as he reads a joke out.

                    LIONEL (CONT'D)
          Move, rock back and forth on the
          balls of your feet, keep the
          movement continuous and flowing.

                                        CUT TO:

Bertie stands framed by the open window.

                         LIONEL (CONT'D)
              I want you to release the five
              vowel sounds, each to last no less
              than 15 seconds.

                         BERTIE
              Aaaaaaaaaaaaaaaaaaaaaaaa...

                         LIONEL
                    (tapping him on the
                    diaphragm)
              Let's connect the toned diaphragm
              with your relaxed throat. Ma'am,
              would you be so kind as to be the
              timekeeper?

Lionel hands her a stop watch.

                         BERTIE
              ....aaaaaaaaaaaaaaaaaaaaaaaa.....

High up in the wall at the back of the building, a Harley
Street physician peers out the window.

                         LIONEL
              Anyone who can vibrate loudly in
              full view of the world can learn to
              give a speech.

                         ELIZABETH
              That's right, Bertie.
                    (checking watch) Now
              Eeeeeeeeeeeeeeeeeeeeeeeeeeeeeeee...

Lionel joins in.

                         LIONEL
              Eeeeeeeeeeeeeeeeeeeeeee.....

                         BERTIE
              Eeeeeeeeeeeeeeeeeeeeeee.....

The sound of "eeee" becomes the roar of machinery

31   INT. MIDLAND FACTORY - NEW DAY   31

Huge industrial wheels whir noisily in neutral as WORKERS
line up dutifully to hear the visiting Royal. Bertie's lips
move, but due to the racket he cannot be heard. Elizabeth
watches in relief.

A FOREMAN, trying to be helpful, signals. The machinery halts, the factory falls silent. At first, the momentum of speaking without being heard carries Bertie forward.

> BERTIE
> I assure you that my wife and I...

Hearing his own voice reverberate through the cavernous factory Bertie's stammer returns.

> BERTIE (CONT'D)
> ...ar-ar-are glad to vis-vis-visit...

Bertie pauses. Takes a breath. Relaxes.

> BERTIE (CONT'D)
> ...are glad to visit this important manufacturing district and see for ourselves one or two of the industries which have made it famous...

He gets back into his stride, despite the silence. Bertie relaxes a little. From Elizabeth, a huge smile of relief.

The sound of an approaching aircraft engine.

32   EXT.   PRIVATE LANDING STRIP, SANDRINGHAM ESTATE - NEW DAY 32

Bertie waits beside a shooting break, a stiff breeze whipping his coat, as a small plane lands and taxis.

While he waits Bertie practises breathing exercises.

The cockpit canopy slides back and - DAVID - leaps out, removing his leather helmet and goggles, gold hair gleaming, a sun god descended from the skies.

> DAVID
> Hello, Bertie. Been waiting long?

> BERTIE
> Where've you been?

Bertie stammers badly in the presence of his brother.

> DAVID
> Been busy.

> BERTIE
> So was I. Elizabeth has pneumonia.

                    DAVID
          I'm sorry. She'll recover.

Bertie shoots him a look.

                    BERTIE
          Father won't.

                    DAVID
          I'll drive.

33   INT./EXT. CAR (SHOOTING BREAK) ON SANDRINGHAM LANE -   33
     CONTINUOUS

David drives. Badly.

                    DAVID
          Old bugger's doing this on purpose.

                    BERTIE
          Dying?

The vehicle almost careens off the lane. Bertie grabs the
wheel and straightens it.

                    DAVID
          Departing prematurely to complicate
          matters.

                    BERTIE
          Oh for heaven's sake, David. You
          know how long he's been ill.

                    DAVID
          Wallis explained. She's terribly
          clever.

34   INT. KING'S BEDROOM, SANDRINGHAM - DAY   34

The King is propped up in his armchair, wrapped in his
favorite faded Tibetan dressing gown. He's attended by six
members of his Privy Council - ARCHBISHOP LANG, LORD DAWSON
his personal physician, LORD WIGRAM his private secretary,
together with RAMSAY MACDONALD, LORD HAILSHAM and SIR JOHN
SIMON. Also present is SIR MAURICE HANKEY, the Clerk to the
Council.

The King's sons and daughter are in attendance. SISTER BLACK
his nurse, stands beside the King.

Lord Wigram is reading out the Order for the Council for the State. The King constantly interjects. He is confused and frail.

> LORD WIGRAM
> ... whereas by letters patent under the Great Seal, bearing date of Westminster, the eleventh June 1912 his Majesty King George V did constitute, order and declare that there should be a guardian, Custos Regni, in the form of Councillors of State.

Off King George V's confusion –

> LORD WIGRAM (CONT'D)
> It's the order of the Council for the State, Sir. So we may act on your behalf.

Wigram presents a tray with papers and pen.

> KING GEORGE V
> I'm still confused...

> LORD WIGRAM
> Approved.

> KING GEORGE V
> Thank you.

Lord Dawson holds the pen as the King makes his 'mark'.

> NURSE
> Feeling a little better Sir?

> KING GEORGE V
> No. I'm not feeling any better. I feel dreadful.

Queen Mary enters.

> KING GEORGE V (CONT'D)
> Have you been skating?

> QUEEN MARY
> No, George.

35   INT. LIBRARY, SANDRINGHAM – CONTINUOUS   35

David is on the phone. Bertie enters.

                    DAVID
          I'm on with Wallis!
               (continues as though
               Bertie didn't exist)
          I know, darling, a talk, even a
          lovely long talk, is a poor
          substitute for holding tight and
          making drowsy. Nor making our own
          drowsies either, as we've had to do
          far too often lately.
               (kisses the phone and
               hangs up)
          Wallis misses me terribly.

                    BERTIE
          Mother says you're late for dinner.

David glares at a clock.

                    DAVID
          She forgets Papa's bloody clocks
          were always half an hour fast!

He sets it back.

36   INT. DINING HALL, SANDRINGHAM - CONTINUOUS   36

David enters and sits between Lord Dawson and Archbishop
Lang.

                    DAVID
               (to Dawson)
          How is my father? I hope he is not
          in pain.

                    LORD DAWSON
          No, no, he's quieter now.

The butler enters and whispers to Lord Dawson and Lord
Wigram. They both exit.

                    QUEEN MARY
          If your father were well, tardiness
          would not be tolerated. None of
          this..unpleasantness would be
          tolerated

Pause.

                    COSMO LANG
              (to David)
          You know Sir, I appreciate that you
          are different from your father in
          your outlook and temperament. I
          want you to know that whenever the
          King questioned your conduct, I
          tried in your interest to present
          it in a most favourable light.

                    DAVID
              (ironic)
          I can always trust you to have my
          best interests at heart.

Awkward silence.

                    QUEEN MARY
          All my children, at the same table.

                    GEORGE
          Yes, Mama.

Lord Wigram enters and whispers to Queen Mary.

                    QUEEN MARY
          It seems our vigil will not be of
          long duration.

INT. KING'S BEDROOM, SANDRINGHAM - NIGHT

Lord Dawson closes the King's eyes.

                    COSMO LANG
          We commend our brother George to
          the mercy of God, our Maker and
          Redeemer.

Queen Mary takes her eldest son's hand and kisses it. Then
Bertie the same.

                    QUEEN MARY
          Long live the King.

                    DAVID
              (very emotional)
          I hope I will make good as he has
          made good.

David falls into his mother's arms, sobbing.

He runs from the room.

37   INT.   CORRIDOR OUTSIDE KING'S BEDROOM - NIGHT   37

David stands, smoking. Bertie comes from the bedroom to
comfort him. David looks broken-hearted.

                    BERTIE
          What on earth was that?

                    DAVID
          Poor Wallis. Now I'm trapped!

38   INT.   LOGUE'S CONSULTATION ROOM - NEW DAY   38

Lionel is at his desk listening to the radio. A news reader
is talking about the death of King George V.

Two of his sons sprawl on the floor. Valentine is studying
for the School Certificate. Antony, the youngest, is taking
a break from homework, building a model airplane.

He switches off the wireless.

                    ANTONY
          Dad?

                    LIONEL
          What?

                    ANTONY
          Time for a Shake, dad?

                    LIONEL
               (flattered)
          You sure? Allright put your
          thinking caps on.

                    VALENTINE
               (looking up from his book)
          Go on, Dad.

This was, and still is, a much loved ritual. Lionel
disappears behind a door..

                    ANTONY
          Bet its the Scottish Play.

                    VALENTINE
          No, I bet it's Othello. It's always
          Othello.

                    LIONEL (OOMING OUT)
          "Art thou afeard?"

                    VALENTINE
               (Without even looking up)
          Caliban!

                    LIONEL
          Oh! For heaven's sake.. that was a
          lucky guess!

                    ANTONY
          Don't listen to egghead. Go on,
          Dad.

Lionel has a pillow stuffed into his jacket to create a
monstrous hunchback. His acting, performed just for his lads,
is quite magical.

                    LIONEL
          "Be not afeard; the isle is full of
          noises,
          Sounds and sweet airs, that give
          delight, and hurt not. Sometimes a
          thousand twanging instruments
          Will hum about mine ears; and
          sometimes voices,
          That, if then I had waked after
          long sleep,
          Will make me sleep again:" (to
          Valentine) Alright, clever clogs,
          what comes next?

                    VALENTINE
          "..and then, in dreaming, The
          clouds methought would open, and
          show riches Ready to drop upon me;
          that..."

                    LIONEL
               (overlapping)
          ...when I waked, I cried to dream
          again." It's such a sad thought.

A KNOCK at the door. Lionel is not expecting anyone.

                    LIONEL (CONT'D)
          Next patient must be early. You
          better go lads, I'm sorry.
               (to the door)
          Won't be a moment, Clifford.

39   INT. WAITING ROOM TO LOGUE'S CHAMBERS - CONTINUOUS   39

The door opens. Bertie is on the other side.

The two men stare at each other, not sure what to say.

>   LIONEL
>   Bertie, they told me not to expect
>   you.
>   (beat)
>   Sorry about your father.

>   BERTIE
>   I don't wish to intrude..
>   (gesturing towards the
>   consultation room)
>   May I?

>   LIONEL
>   Of course. Please come in.

>   BERTIE
>   I've been practising. One hour a
>   day. In spite of everything.
>   (notices Lionel's hump)
>   What's going on there?

>   LIONEL
>   I was, sorry, mucking around with
>   my kids.

Lionel hastily removes the pillow, tossing it away. Realizes
Bertie has entered the consultation room.

40   INT. LOGUE'S CONSULTATION ROOM - CONTINUOUS   40

>   LIONEL
>   Do you feel like working today?

Bertie notices the plane left behind by Logue's sons.

>   BERTIE
>   A Curtis bi-plane.

>   LOGUE
>   I'll put on some hot milk.

>   BERTIE
>   Logue, I'd kill for something
>   stronger.

>   LIONEL
>   I wasn't there for my father's
>   death. Still makes me sad.

>   BERTIE
>   I can imagine so.

Lionel passes Bertie a brandy.

> BERTIE (CONT'D)
> What did you father do?

> LIONEL
> A brewer.

> BERTIE
> Oh.

> LIONEL
> At least there was free beer.

Pause.

> LIONEL (CONT'D)
> Here's to the memory of your
> father.

They sit.

> BERTIE
> I was informed, after the fact, my
> father's last words were: "Bertie
> has more guts than the rest of his
> brothers put together." He couldn't
> say that to my face.

Silence.

> BERTIE (CONT'D)
> (blurts)
> My brother. That's why I'm here.

> LIONEL
> What's he done?

> BERTIE
> Can't say. I can't puh-puh-puh...

His jaw and throat muscles constrict.

> LIONEL
> Try singing it.

> BERTIE
> Pardon?

> LIONEL
> Know any songs?

> BERTIE
> Songs?

>   LIONEL
> Yes songs.

>   BERTIE
> "Swanee River".

>   LIONEL
> I love that song.

>   BERTIE
> Happens to be my favorite.

>   LIONEL
> Sing it then. Give me the chorus.

>   BERTIE
> No. Certainly not.
>   (fascinated by the plane)
> Always wanted to build models.
> Father wouldn't allow it. *He*
> collected stamps. I had to collect
> stamps.

>   LIONEL
> You can finish that off.

Bertie eagerly reaches for some balsa.

>   LIONEL (CONT'D)
> *If* you sing.
>   (to "Swanee River")
> *"When I was a boy with David...upon*
> *the Swanee River."*

>   BERTIE
> I can't sit here singing!

>   LIONEL
> You can with me.

>   BERTIE
> Because you're peculiar.

>   LIONEL
> I take that as a compliment.

>   BERTIE
> I'm not crooning "Swanee River!"

>   LIONEL
> Try "Camptown Races" then.
>   (sings)
>   (MORE)

                    LIONEL (CONT'D)
          "My brother D, he said to me, doo-
          dah doo-dah..." Continuous sound
          will give you flow. Does it feel
          strange, now that David's on the
          throne?

                    BERTIE
          It was a relief... Knowing I
          wouldn't be King.

Reaches into his jacket for his cigarette case. Then
remembers, puts it away.

                    LIONEL
          But unless he produces an heir,
          you're next in line. And your
          daughter, Elizabeth, would then
          succeed you.

                    BERTIE
          "You're barking up the wrong tree
          now, Doctor, Doctor."

                    LIONEL
          "Lionel, Lionel." You didn't
          stammer.

                    BERTIE
          Of course I didn't stammer, I was
          singing!
               (realises)
          Oh...

                    LIONEL
          Well, as a little reward, you get
          to put some glue on these struts.

                    BERTIE
          David and I were very close. Young
          bucks... You know.

                    LIONEL
          Chase the same girls?

                    BERTIE
          David was always very helpful in
          arranging introductions. We shared
          the expert ministrations of
          "Paulette" in Paris. Not at the
          same time of course.

An uncomfortable silence. Too much has been said.

                    LIONEL
          Did David tease you?

                    BERTIE
          They all did. "Buh-buh-buh-Bertie".
          Father encouraged it. "Get it out,
          boy!" Said it would make me stop.
          Said..."I was afraid of my father,
          and my children are damn well going
          to be afraid of me".

Lionel has been watching Bertie work on the model.

                    LIONEL
          Naturally right handed?

                    BERTIE
          Left. I was punished. Now I use the
          right.

                    LIONEL
          Yes, that's very common with
          stammerers. Anything other
          corrections?

                    BERTIE
          Knock knees.

Lionel waits.

                    BERTIE (CONT'D)
          Metal splints were made...worn
          night and day.

                    LIONEL
          That must have been painful.

                    BERTIE
          Bloody agony. Straight legs now.

                    LIONEL
          Who were you closest to in your
          family?

                    BERTIE
          Nannies. Not my first nanny,
          though..she loved David...hated me.
          When I was presented to my parents
          for the daily viewing, she'd...

The stammering produced by the memory halts him.

                    LIONEL
          Sing it.

                              BERTIE
                        (tunelessly)
                  "She pinch me so I'd cry,
                  and be sent away at once,
                  then she wouldn't feed me, far far
                  away."
                        (speaks)
                  Took three years for my parents to
                  notice. As you can imagine, it
                  caused some stomach problems.
                  Still.

                              LIONEL
                  What about your brother Johnnie?
                  Were you close to him?

                              BERTIE
                  Sweet boy. Epilepsy...and...he
                  was 'different'. Died at 13, hidden
                  from view. Too embarrassing for the
                  family.
                        (nervous)
                  I've been told it's not catching.

                              LIONEL
                  Do you want a top-up?

                              BERTIE
                  Please.

Lionel gets up to pour another drink.

                              BERTIE (CONT'D)
                  You know, Lionel, you're the first
                  ordinary Englishman...

                              LIONEL
                  Australian.

                              BERTIE
                  ...I've ever really spoken to.
                  Sometimes, when I ride through the
                  streets and see, you know, the
                  Common Man staring at me, I'm
                  struck by how little I know of his
                  life, and how little he knows of
                  mine.

                              LIONEL
                  What're friends for.

                              BERTIE
                  I wouldn't know.

41   ARCHIVE FOOTAGE OF KING GEORGE V'S STATE FUNERAL   41

The common man, and woman, en masse. Thousands of them, solemn in their bereavement.

Funereal bagpipes wail, joining the measured drum-rolls.

Ranks upon ranks of military personnel slow-stepping the ceremonial death march.

Muffled cannons bark their salute.

Startled, a large flock of blackbirds rise up and streak across the wintery sky.

A Naval squad pulls a gun carriage that carries the King's coffin draped with the Royal standard, on which rests the Royal crown topped by a jeweled Maltese Cross.

On Whitehall, the gun carriage passes the Cenotaph.

                  PATHE NEWSREEL ANNOUNCER
         All salute as they pass the
         Cenotaph. One million died for
         him...as King George died for them.

We see naval cadets salute to their right.

END ARCHIVE FOOTAGE.

42   EXT. WHITEHALL - DAY   42

David, very solemn, Bertie - pale and fragile, their brothers Henry and George all salute as they pass the Cenotaph.

The crowd is silent.

Lionel, Myrtle, and all three boys are part of the crowd, half a dozen rows back. Antony and Valentine have mirrors on sticks to see over the heads.

                  LIONEL
         (whispers a running
          commentary to the boys)
        That's the Prince of Wales. He's
        now King because he's the oldest.

Lionel spots...

Bertie, in the procession passing by.

Lionel stares at him. Tries to make eye contact. In the midst
of this pomp and ceremony the immense potential importance of
his client sinks in. Of course, Bertie doesn't see him.

                    LIONEL (CONT'D)
          Quite an irony...all this.

                    MYRTLE
          Why's that?

                    LIONEL
          His children weren't too fond of
          him.

                    MYRTLE
          Lionel! What a thing to say.
          Where'd you pick that up?

                    LIONEL
          Heard it...at work.

Lionel points, to distract.

                    LIONEL (CONT'D)
          Think the German will make it?

Return to archive footage, a contorted limping German is
seen. The procession of dignitaries continues.

                    PATHE NEWSREEL ANNOUNCER
          ....fifteen Kings of Europe and
          eleven Princes of the Realm are
          here...

43   EXT. AUSTIN DRIVING THRU SCOTTISH ESTATE - NEW DAY   43

                    BERTIE (O.S.)
          "I sifted seven thick-stalked
          thistles through strong thick
          sieves. I sifted seven..."

                    ELIZABETH (O.S.)
          Bertie, isn't that enough?

                    BERTIE (O.S.)
          I have to keep saying it. This is
          your fault.

CHOP! CHOP! CHOP! The sound of an axe.

Fallen trees start to litter the roadside.

44   INT. AUSTIN, ROYAL COUNTRY ESTATE - CONTINUOUS   44

Bertie and Elizabeth are dressed for a party. Outside, fallen
trees, and more falling. They're aghast.

> ELIZABETH
> Five hundred year old
> oaks...removed to improve the view!

> BERTIE
> Nonetheless...we *must* try to be
> pleasant towards Mrs Simpson.

> ELIZABETH
> You know she calls me "The Fat
> Scottish Cook"?

> BERTIE
> You're not fat.

> ELIZABETH
> I'm getting plump.

> BERTIE
> You seldom cook.

She gives her husband a look, but realizes he's teasing. She
gasps and points:

POV - more trees being felled.

> BERTIE (CONT'D)
> I sifted seven.

> ELIZABETH
> Shut up!!

45   INT. BALLROOM, BALMORAL - DAY   45

A weekend house party. Drinks at teatime. Five or six friends
dance to a gramophone. A couple are already drunk. At the
epicenter, David, the very picture of insouciance, and
WALLIS, clinging to his arm, dripping in jewelry. Wallis'
most attractive physical feature is her back, displayed fully
by her choice of dress. Surrounded by their entourage, they
are the apex of chic.

A FOOTMAN announces:

> FOOTMAN
> Their Royal Highnesses the Duke and
> Duchess of York.

Elizabeth freezes as Wallis sweeps forward to greet them.

> WALLIS
> How lovely to see you both. Welcome
> to our little country shack.

Elizabeth stares at her, incredulous, then sails past,
announcing to no one in particular:

> ELIZABETH
> I came at the invitation of the
> King.

Wallis is wrongfooted. Elizabeth and Bertie reach David.
Elizabeth curtsies to David, and Bertie gives David a nod.

> BERTIE
> Hello David.

> DAVID
> Hello Bertie. Hello Elizabeth.

David kisses Elizabeth on both cheeks.

> BERTIE
> I see you're making some changes to
> the garden.

> DAVID
> I am. I am not quite finished.

David's eyes are drawn by Wallis.

> WALLIS
> David!

She taps her champagne glass.

A footman goes into action, but Wallis waves him off. David
leaves instead.

> DAVID
> (calling to Wallis)
> Just be a sec, darling!

Bertie pursues him.

One of the guests - WINSTON CHURCHILL - nursing a glass of
champagne moves up to Elizabeth.

46   INT. DRAWING ROOM/PORTRAIT GALLERY, BALMORAL - DAY   46

Elizabeth is standing in front of a canvas of George IV when Churchill arrives at her side.

> ELIZABETH
> Don't tell me I behaved badly, Mr Churchill.

> WINSTON CHURCHILL
> On the contrary, your Royal Highness. Etiquette decrees royalty must be greeted by the official host: in this case: the King. Not a commoner. You behaved impeccably. As always.

> ELIZABETH
> Thank you.

> WINSTON CHURCHILL
> I'm always amused when you're referred to as being a commoner. As common as the Scottish kings from whom you descend.

> ELIZABETH
> Your flattery is profound. What is your agenda, Mr Churchill?

> WINSTON CHURCHILL
> (pause, then)
> Did she actually say what I thought she said?

> ELIZABETH
> You know she did.

> WINSTON CHURCHILL
> What is her hold on him?

> ELIZABETH
> Apparently she has certain...skills, which she learnt in an establishment in Shanghai.

Churchill almost spills his new champagne.

> WINSTON CHURCHILL
> Mam, I'd not realized you were so well versed in such matters.

They catch a distant glimpse of David hurrying down a corridor, followed by Bertie, determined to catch up.

47   INT. CORRIDOR, BALMORAL - CONTINUOUS   47

Bertie catches his brother.

                    BERTIE
          I've been trying to see you...

                    DAVID
          I've been terribly busy.

                    BERTIE
          Doing what?

                    DAVID
          Kinging.

                    BERTIE
          Really? Kinging? Kinging is a
          precarious business! Where is the
          Tsar of Russia? Where is Cousin
          Wilhelm?

                    DAVID
          You're being dreary.

                    BERTIE
          Is Kinging laying off eighty staff
          at Sandringham and buying yet more
          pearls for Wallis while there are
          people marching across Europe
          singing "The Red Flag"?

                    DAVID
          Stop your worrying. Herr Hitler
          will sort that lot out.

                    BERTIE
          Who'll sort out Herr Hitler?

David hurries down some stairs.

48   INT. SERVANT'S CORRIDOR/WINE CELLAR - DAY   48

David is hunting for a bottle of champagne for Wallis in the
wine cellar.

                    BERTIE
          And you've put that woman into our
          mother's suite?

                    DAVID
          Mother's not still in the bed, is
          she?

>   BERTIE
>   That's not funny.

David finds the bottle he was looking for.

>   DAVID
>   Wally likes the very best.

>   BERTIE
>   I don't care what woman you carry
>   on with at night, as long as you
>   show up for duty in the morning!

He exits. Bertie follows.

49   INT. HALLWAY BALMORAL - DAY   49

>   DAVID
>   This is not just some woman I am
>   carrying on with. This is the woman
>   I intend to marry

>   BERTIE
>   Excuse me?

>   DAVID
>   She's filing a petition for
>   divorce.

>   BERTIE
>   Good God.

50   INT. HALLWAY/DRAWING ROOM, BALMORAL - DAY   50

>   BERTIE
>   Can't you just give her a nice
>   house and a title?

>   DAVID
>   I won't have her as my mistress.

>   BERTIE
>   David, the Church does not
>   recognise divorce and you are the
>   head of the Church.

>   DAVID
>   Haven't I any rights?

>   BERTIE
>   Many privileges...

                    DAVID
        Not the same thing. Your beloved
        Common Man may marry for love, why
        not me?

                    BERTIE
        If you were the Common Man, on what
        basis could you possibly claim to
        be King?!

                    DAVID
        Sounds like you've studied our
        wretched constitution.

                    BERTIE
        Sounds like you haven't.

                    DAVID
        Is that what this is all about? Is
        that why you've been taking
        elocution lessons?

                    BERTIE
        I'm attempting t-t...

                    DAVID
        That's the scoop around town.
        Yearning for a larger audience are
        we, B-b-b-bertie?

                    BERTIE
        D-don't say such a th-

                    DAVID
        Young brother trying to push older
        brother off throne...Positively
        medieval.

                    BERTIE
        D-

Bertie is completely locked.

David heads for Wallis, leaving his brother totally
distraught. He pours her a glass of champagne. She shows she
is pleased with him.

51   INT. LOGUE'S CONSULTATION ROOM, HARLEY STREET - NEW DAY   51

Bertie stands shattered, lost in painful memory.

                    BERTIE
          All that work, down the drain. My
          own brother... I couldn't say...I
          could say...I couldn't say a word
          in reply!

                    LIONEL
          Why do you stammer more with David
          than you do with me?

                    BERTIE
          Because you're bloody well paid to
          listen!

The latter, angry, sentence is flawless.

                    LIONEL
          I'm not a geisha girl.

                    BERTIE
          Stop trying to be so bloody clever!

                    LIONEL
          What is it about David that stops
          you speaking?

                    BERTIE
          What the bloody hell is it that
          makes you bloody well want to go on
          about David?

                    LIONEL
          Vulgar but fluent. You don't
          stammer when you swear.

                    BERTIE
          Bugger off!

                    LIONEL
          Is that the best you can do?

                    BERTIE
          Well bloody bugger to you, you
          beastly bastard.

                    LIONEL
          A public school prig can do better
          than that.

                    BERTIE
          Shit then. Shit, shit, shit!

                    LIONEL
        See how defecation flows trippingly
        from the tongue?

                    BERTIE
        Because I'm angry!

                    LIONEL
        Ah. Know the f-word?

                    BERTIE
        Fornication?

                    LIONEL
        Bertie.

Lionel gives him a look.

                    BERTIE
        Fuck. Fuck, fuck, fuck!

                    LIONEL
        Yes! You see! Not a hesitation!

                    BERTIE
        Bloody, bloody, bloody! Shit, shit,
        shit! Bugger, bugger, bugger! Fuck,
        fuck, fuck!

A knocking on the wall.

                    ANTONY (O.S.)
        Dad? What's going on?

                    LIONEL
            (calls)
        Sorry. Finish your homework.

Bertie laughs.

                    LIONEL (CONT'D)
        Well that's a side of you we don't
        get to see that often.

                    BERTIE
        No. No we're not supposed to
        really, not publicly.

                    LIONEL
        Can't joke, can't laugh?
            (then referring to Antony
             on the other side of the
             wall)
        Let's get some air.

> BERTIE
> No Logue, I don't think that's a
> good idea.

Lionel throws him his hat and scarf.

> LIONEL
> Put on your spy clobber.

52   EXT. REGENT'S PARK ORNAMENTAL GARDEN - DAY   52

Bertie and Logue come into view talking. Bertie with his
homburg pulled low, scarf wrapped high. The park is empty and
bleak on this winter's day. One can feel the cold chill;
puffs of steam punctuating their words like smoke signals.

> LIONEL
> What's wrong? What's got you so
> upset?

> BERTIE
> Logue, you have no idea. My brother
> is infatuated with a woman who's
> been married twice - and she's
> American.

> LIONEL
> Some of them must be loveable.

> BERTIE
> (shoots him a look)
> She's asking for a divorce and
> David is determined to marry her.
> Mrs Wallis Simpson of Baltimore.

> LIONEL
> That's not right. Queen Wallis of
> Baltimore?

> BERTIE
> Unthinkable.

> LIONEL
> Can he do that?

> BERTIE
> Absolutely not. But he's going to
> anyway. All hell's broken loose.

> LIONEL
> Can't they carry on privately?

> BERTIE
> If only they would.

> LIONEL
> Where does that leave you?

> BERTIE
> I know my place! I'll do anything
> within my power to keep my brother
> on the throne.

> LIONEL
> Has it come to that? But the way
> things are going, your place may be
> on the throne.

> BERTIE
> I am not an alternative to my
> brother.

> LIONEL
> If you had to you could outshine
> David...

Lionel reaches out and gives Bertie a pat of comfort on the shoulder. Bertie pulls back in offended shock.

> BERTIE
> Don't take liberties! That's
> bordering on treason.

> LIONEL
> I'm just saying you *could* be King.
> You could do it!

> BERTIE
> That *is* treason!

They face each other, as though in combat.

> LIONEL
> I'm trying to get you to realise
> you need not be governed by fear.

> BERTIE
> I've had enough of this!

> LIONEL
> What're you afraid of?

> BERTIE
> Your poisonous words!

                    LIONEL
          Why'd you show up then? To take
          polite elocution lessons so you can
          chit-chat at posh tea parties?

                    BERTIE
          Don't instruct me on my duties! I'm
          the brother of a King...the son of
          a King...we have a history that
          goes back untold centuries. You're
          the disappointing son of a brewer!
          A jumped-up jackeroo from the
          outback! You're nobody. These
          sessions are over!

Bertie strides off in a fury. Lionel, equally angry, goes in
the other direction. Two men moving apart in the cold
wintery landscape, the ground mist rising.

The Lionel stops. Turns.

POV - Bertie has disappeared from view.

CLOSE ON LIONEL as he realises...he's no longer therapist to
a man who might have to become King.

53   EXT. BACK GARDEN ENTRANCE, 10 DOWNING STREET/HORSE GUARDS 53
       PARADE - DAY

       A car pulls up. A bundled figure hurries out and slips in
       thru the garden entrance.

54   INT. BALDWIN'S STUDY, 10 DOWNING STREET - DAY   54

       Bertie is with Prime Minister STANLEY BALDWIN, a stocky man
       with his hair parted straight down the middle. Their
       conversation in progress.

                    BALDWIN
          It's not just because she's an
          American. It's that she is soon to
          be a twice divorced American, and
          the King can not marry a divorced
          woman. I apologize for the nature
          of this, but... according to
          Scotland Yard, the King does not
          possess exclusive rights to Mrs.
          Simpson's favours and affections,
          sharing them with a married used
          car salesman, a certain Mr Guy
          Trundle.
                    (MORE)

                          BALDWIN (CONT'D)
              In addition, it is rumoured that
              Hitler's ambassador, Count von
              Ribbentrop, sends her 17 carnations
              every day......

Silence.

                          BALDWIN (CONT'D)
              Should your brother continue to
              ignore the advice of His
              Government, He must abdicate.
              Otherwise His Government has no
              choice but to resign.

                          BERTIE
              Prime Minister, you'd leave the
              country without a government?

                          BALDWIN
              Does the King do what he wants, or
              does he do what his people expect
              him to do?

55   INT. LIVING ROOM, LOGUE APARTMENT - NIGHT   55

        The family is listening to a favorite radio show.

                          MYRTLE
              What's the matter, love?

                          LIONEL
              Nothing.

        Lionel shrugs helplessly, glances at the boys.

                          MYRTLE
              You look a bit blue.

                          LIONEL
              Just trouble with a client.

                          MYRTLE
              Oh yes.

                          LIONEL
              Frightened of his own shadow.

                          MYRTLE
              Isn't that why they come to you?

                          LIONEL
              But this chap...

                    MYRTLE
          Yes?

                    LIONEL
          This chap truly could be somebody
          great, and he's fighting me.

                    MYRTLE
          Perhaps he doesn't want to be
          great.

Lionel is silent.

                    MYRTLE (CONT'D)
          Perhaps that's what you want.

                    LIONEL
          I might have overstepped the mark.

                    MYRTLE
          Apologize, Lionel. Do you both
          good. Sometimes you do push a bit
          hard.

56   INT. HALLWAY, 145 PICCADILLY - CONTINUOUS   56

Lionel is shown to a chair in the hall to wait. Footsteps
echo.

Bertie's Equerry, dressed in military uniform, comes in. He
is scrupulously polite.

                    EQUERRY
          I'm very sorry, Mr Logue, the Duke
          is terrible busy.

                    LIONEL
          I'm happy to wait. Or I could come
          back later.

                    EQUERRY
          As I said, the Duke is busy.

The steward opens the door. Both wait.

Lionel reluctantly withdraws.

57   INT. BERTIE'S STUDY, 145 PICCADILLY - NIGHT   57

Bertie and Chuchill sit on either side of Bertie's desk.

> WINSTON CHURCHILL
> But there were other reasons for
> concern, Sir. He was careless with
> state papers. He lacked commitment
> and resolve. There were those that
> worried where he would stand when
> war with Germany comes.

> BERTIE
> We're not coming to that?

> WINSTON CHURCHILL
> Indeed we are, Sir. Prime Minister
> Baldwin may deny this, but Hitler's
> intent is crystal clear. War with
> Germany will come, and we will need
> a King behind whom we can all stand
> united.

Silence.

> WINSTON CHURCHILL (CONT'D)
> Have you thought what you will call
> yourself?

Bertie struggles to speak with the shock of the question.

> WINSTON CHURCHILL (CONT'D)
> Certainly not Albert, Sir. Too
> Germanic.

Pause.

> WINSTON CHURCHILL (CONT'D)
> What about George? After your
> father? George the sixth. It has
> rather a nice continuity to it,
> don't you think.

58   INT.   DAVID'S DRAWING ROOM, THE FORT - DAY   58

Bertie waits nervously for David.

David enters, looking sunken.

> BERTIE
> David! Thank God. You look
> exhausted! How are you bearing up?

> DAVID
> Bertie. I have to go. The
> decision's been made.

                    BERTIE
          I cannot accept that. You are in no
          condition to make that decision.

                    DAVID
          I'm afraid there's no other way. I
          must marry her. My mind's made up.
          I'm... sorry.

                    BERTIE
          That's a terrible thing to hear.
          David, nobody wants that. I least
          of all.

59   INT. - DRAWING ROOM, THE FORT - DAY   59

                    DAVID (V.O. RADIO FILTER)
          At long last I am able to say a few
          words of my own. I have never
          wanted to withhold anything, but
          until now, it has not been
          constitutionally possible for me to
          speak. A few hours ago I discharged
          my last duty as King and Emperor.
          Now that I have been succeeded by
          my brother, the Duke of York my
          first words must be to declare my
          allegiance to him. This I do with
          all my heart.

Bertie, Henry and George are there to witness David signing
the abdication document.

Silence. The scratching of a fountain pen.

He finally signs his name. The others sign.

Bertie signs.

HOLD ON Bertie's face.

60   INT. STUDY, WINDSOR CASTLE - NIGHT   60

David sits at his desk on which sits a BBC microphone. As
always he speaks with beautiful fluency.

                    DAVID (V.O. RADIO FILTER)
          You all know the reasons which have
          impelled me to renounce the throne.
                    (MORE)

                        DAVID (V.O. RADIO FILTER) (CONT'D)
                    But you must believe me when I tell
                    you I have found it impossible to
                    carry the heavy burden of
                    responsibility and to discharge my
                    duties as King as I would wish to
                    do without the help and support of
                    the woman I love...

61   INT. DRAWING ROOM, YORK HOUSE - NIGHT   61

ANOTHER WIRELESS being listened to by Elizabeth and Bertie.

                        DAVID (V.O. RADIO FILTER)
                    ..This decision has been made less
                    difficult to me by the sure
                    knowledge that my brother, with his
                    long training in the public affairs
                    of this country...

Bertie battles his emotions. Elizabeth takes Bertie's hand
supportively.

62   INT. HALLWAY. 145 PICCADILLY - NEW DAY   62

Bertie is in full regalia of an Admiral of the Fleet's
uniform.

                        DAVID (V.O. RADIO FILTER)
                    ...and with his fine qualities...

63   EXT. 145 PICCADILLY - CONTINUOUS   63

                        DAVID (V.O. RADIO FILTER)
                    ...will be able to take my place
                    forthwith without interruption or
                    injury to the life and progress of
                    the empire.

Grimly, Bertie gets in to a waiting Rolls. Framed in the car
window he looks terrified as the car edges from the curb.

On the pavement, kept back by police, a crowd of onlookers.
On the edge of the group...Lionel.

Bertie peers out of the window of the Rolls. Their eyes meet.
Bertie looks away. The Rolls drives on.

64   INT. ANTECHAMBER, ST JAMES PALACE - THAT DAY   64

Bertie waits nervously.

At a signal from his attendants he enters the Accession
Council Chamber

65   INT. ACCESSION COUNCIL CHAMBER - CONTINUOUS   65

The Council is made up of Privy Councillors, members of the
House of Lords,. the Lord Mayor of the City of London, the
Aldermen of the City of London and the High Commissioners of
some Commonwealth countries.

Standing before them, Bertie is handed his Accession speech.

All of Bertie's old symptoms reappear: the tightening of the
neck muscles, the protruding Adam's apple, the jaw locking.

>   BERTIE
> I meet you today in circumstances
> which are -

Bertie has come to a complete muscle-locked halt. He bows his
head in humility. And shame.

66   INT. HALLWAY, YORK HOUSE - THAT DAY   66

Elizabeth is with her daughters, preparing for the move to
Buckingham Palace. The girls are tidying away their toy
horses.

>   LILLIBET
> Mama, will we have space for our
> horses in our new home?

>   ELIZABETH
> Of course we will, darling, we'll
> have a palace of rooms.

Bertie appears, still in full regalia, straight from the
Accession Council. He tries to put on a brave front, but it
doesn't quite work. He desperately needs the comfort of his
family.

He holds his arm out, expecting his daughters to run to him
for a hug and kiss, his solace after the ordeal.

>   LILLIBET
> (to her sister, on seeing
>   her father)
> Curtsey.

>   MARGARET
> Your Majesty.

They remain where they are and curtsy formally. Bertie is devastated.

>   ELIZABETH
>   How was it?

Bertie shakes his head imperceptibly.

67   INT. BERTIE'S STUDY, YORK HOUSE - NIGHT   67

Bertie valiantly tries to make sense of his new dispatch box filled with state papers, seated at his desk. It is late at night.

Elizabeth enters, in night clothes.

>   BERTIE
>   I'm trying to familiarise myself
>   with what a state paper looks like.

He picks up a series of papers.

>   BERTIE (CONT'D)
>   A despatch from Mr Baldwin which I
>   don't understand a word of. David's
>   finances. The Christmas broadcast -
>   I think that might be a mistake.

>   ELIZABETH
>   Don't do it then.

>   BERTIE
>   Plans for the Coronation - I think
>   that's an even bigger mistake. I'm
>   not a King. I'm a naval officer.
>   Its the only thing I know about.

And Bertie breaks down; fierce, wracking sobs.

Elizabeth speaks softly, with growing strength, having already accepted and adapted to the situation.

>   ELIZABETH
>   Dear, dear man... I refused your
>   first two marriage proposals, not
>   because I didn't love you, but
>   because I couldn't bear the royal
>   cage. Could bear the idea of a life
>   of tours and public duties, a life
>   that no longer was really to be my
>   own. Then I thought...he stammers
>   so beautifully...they'll leave us
>   alone.

She takes his anguished face in her hands tenderly.

>   ELIZABETH (CONT'D)
>   But if I must be Queen, I intend be
>   a very good Queen. Queen to a very
>   great King indeed.

68   EXT. LOGUE HOME, SOUTH KENSINGTON - NEW DAY   68

Re-establishing shot. Two large cars wait at the curb-side.

69   INT. PARLOUR, LOGUE APARTMENT - CONTINUOUS   69

A knock at the front door.

Two figures can be seen outlined in the frosted glass door.

Lionel opens it.

Bertie and Elizabeth are standing there.

>   BERTIE
>   Waiting for a king to apologize,
>   one can wait rather a long wait.

>   ELIZABETH
>   I'm afraid we're slightly late.

Beat.

>   LIONEL
>   This is home. Myrtle's at bridge.
>   I've made sure the boys are out.

>   ELIZABETH
>   (stepping in)
>   It's lovely. Absolutely lovely.

Lionel pulls out a chair for her to sit down.

>   LIONEL
>   Would you like some tea, Ma'am?

>   ELIZABETH
>   Yes. I'll help myself.
>   (then)
>   Off you go now. Or must I knock
>   your heads together?

The two men enter and sit down. A moment of uncertainty. Then
Bertie blurts.

> BERTIE
> Here's your shilling, Logue
> (puts shilling down)
> I understand what you were trying
> to say, Logue.

> LIONEL
> I went about it the wrong way. I'm
> sorry.

> BERTIE
> Now here I am. Is the nation ready
> for two minutes of radio silence?

> LIONEL
> Every stammerer always fears they
> will fall back to square one. I
> don't let that happen. You won't
> let that happen.

> BERTIE
> If I fail in my duty... David could
> come back. I've seen the placards
> "Save Our King!" They don't mean
> me. Every other monarch in history
> succeeded someone who was dead, or
> about to be. My predecessor is not
> only alive, but very much so. What
> a bloody mess! I can't even give
> them a Christmas Speech.

> LIONEL
> Like your Dad used to do?

> BERTIE
> Precisely.

> LIONEL
> Your father. He's not here.

> BERTIE
> Yes he is. He's on that bloody
> shilling I gave you.

> LIONEL
> Easy enough to give away. You don't
> have to carry him around in your
> pocket. Or your brother.
> (MORE)

> LIONEL (CONT'D)
> You don't need to be afraid of
> things you were afraid of when you
> were five.

A pause –

> LIONEL (CONT'D)
> You're very much your own man,
> Bertie. Your face is next, mate.

There's a noise outside the door.

> MYRTLE (O.S.)
> Lionel?

> LIONEL
> Myrtle!

Lionel stands and pressed himself up against the wall.

> BERTIE
> Are you alright, Lionel?

> LIONEL
> Yes.

Bertie stands and makes towards the door.

> BERTIE
> Shall we go through?

> LIONEL
> (not moving)
> Trust me it's important.

> BERTIE
> What is it?

71   INT. PARLOUR, LOGUE APARTMENT - CONTINUOUS   71

Myrtle has entered, she is flabbergasted.

> MYRTLE
> Your... your...

> ELIZABETH
> It's "Your Majesty", the first
> time. After that, "Ma'am", as in
> ham, not Ma'lm as in palm.

72   INT. LOGUE'S STUDY - CONTINUOUS   72

Lionel, still pressed against the wall, is explaining his
reticence to Bertie.

                    LIONEL
          I haven't told her.. about us. Sit
          down, relax.

Bertie, bemused, sits.

73   INT. PARLOUR, LOGUE APARTMENT - CONTINUOUS   73

                    ELIZABETH
          I'm informed your husband calls my
          husband Bertie and my husband calls
          your husband Lionel. I trust you
          won't call me Liz.

                    MYRTLE
          Your Majesty, you may call me Mrs
          Logue, Ma'am.

                    ELIZABETH
          Very nice to meet you, Mrs Logue

Myrtle is taken aback.

74   INT. LOGUE'S STUDY - CONTINUOUS   74

The men listen to their wives' conversation.

                    BERTIE
          Logue, we can't stay here all day.

                    LIONEL
          Yes we can.

                    BERTIE
          Logue..

                    LIONEL
          Look, I need to wait for the
          opportune moment.

                    BERTIE
                (realizing)
          You're being a coward!

                    LIONEL
          You're damn right.

Decisive, Bertie stands and throws open the door.

> BERTIE
> Get out there, man!

And Bertie ushers Lionel into the parlour.

75   INT. PARLOUR, LOGUE APARTMENT - CONTINUOUS   75

Logue enters, pretending total innocence and surprise, followed by Bertie.

> LIONEL
> Oh! Hello, Myrtle darling! You're early.(indicating Elizabeth) I believe you two have met! I don't believe you know....King George VI?

> BERTIE
> It's very nice to meet you.

Myrtle stares at Lionel and takes her revenge.

> MYRTLE
> Will their Majesties be staying for dinner?

Logue and Bertie look panic-stricken. Elizabeth comes to the rescue.

> ELIZABETH
> We would love to, such a treat, but alas...a previous engagement. What a pity.

On Lionel's relief.

76   EXT. WESTMINSTER ABBEY - DAY   76

To establish. Preparations are being made in the street for the coronation - spectator stands are complete and fabric is being dressed.

77   INT. WESTMINSTER ABBEY - DAY   77

The center piece of the Coronation staging is the throne of Edward the Confessor. Scaffolding has been erected to supply seating. Technicians work to erect film cameras, lights, radio microphones.

They stop short as they see Cosmo Lang waiting to greet them, flanked by the Dean of Westminster and a couple of flunkies.

There is a distinct drop in temperature.

> BERTIE
> Archbishop.

> COSMO LANG
> Welcome your Majesty.
> (referring to the
> cathedral, but it's
> double-edge)
> What a glorious transformation,
> Sir. I hope you'll forgive us if we
> continue our preparations. Allow me
> to guide you through the ceremony.

They begin to walk together, Lionel a few paces behind.

> COSMO LANG (CONT'D)
> We begin, of course at the West
> Door, then into the nave.

> BERTIE
> I see all your pronouncements are
> to be broadcast, Archbishop.

Cosmo sees Bertie staring at the microphones.

> COSMO LANG
> Ah, yes, wireless is indeed a
> Pandora's Box. I'm afraid I've also
> had to permit the newsreel cameras.
> The product of which I shall
> personally edit.

> LIONEL
> Without momentary hesitation.

> BERTIE
> Doctor Lionel Logue of Harley
> Street, my speech specialist.

> COSMO LANG
> Specialist?! Had I known Your
> Majesty was seeking assistance I
> would've made my own
> recommendation.

> BERTIE
> Dr. Logue is to be present at the
> Coronation.

> COSMO LANG
> Well of course I shall speak to the
> Dean, but it will be extremely
> difficult.

> BERTIE
> I should like the Doctor to be
> seated in the King's Box.

> COSMO LANG
> But members of your Family will be
> seated there, Sir.

> BERTIE
> That why it's suitable.

> LIONEL
> And now, if you don't mind, we need
> the premises.

> COSMO LANG
> My dear fellow, this is Westminster
> Abbey! The Church must prepare his
> Majesty.

> LIONEL
> My preparations for Bertie are
> equally important.

The two men stare each other down.

> LIONEL (CONT'D)
> With complete privacy. If you don't
> mind.

> BERTIE
> Those are my wishes, Your Grace.

> COSMO LANG
>   (sniffs)
> I shall place the Abbey at Your
> Majesty's disposal...this evening.
> Your Majesty.

Lang nods curtly and exits.

78   INT. WESTMINSTER ABBEY - THAT NIGHT   78

Footsteps resonate.

Lionel enters. Ahead, he sees Cosmo Lang quietly conferring
with Bertie. As Lionel approached, Cosmo Lang slips away.

                    LIONEL
          I can't believe I'm walking on
          Chaucer **and** Handel **and** Dickens.
          Everything alright? Let's get
          cracking.

Bertie, seated on a ceremonial chair, does not rise.

                    BERTIE
          I'm not here to rehearse, Doctor
          Logue.

Pause-

                    BERTIE (CONT'D)
          True, you never called yourself
          'Doctor'. I did that for you. No
          diploma, no training, no
          qualifications. Just a great deal
          of nerve.

                    LIONEL
          Ah, the star chamber inquisition,
          is it?

                    BERTIE
          You asked for trust and total
          equality.

                    LIONEL
          Bertie, I heard you at Wembley, I
          was there. I heard you. My son
          Laurie said "Do you think you could
          help that poor man?" I replied "If
          I had the chance".

                    BERTIE
          What, as a failed actor!?

                    LIONEL
          It's true, I'm not a doctor, and
          yes I acted a bit, recited in pubs
          and taught elocution in schools.
          When the Great War came, our boys
          were pouring back from the front,
          shell-shocked and unable to speak
          and somebody said, "Lionel, you're
          very good at all this speech stuff.
          Do you think you could possibly
          help these poor buggers". I did
          muscle therapy, exercise,
          relaxation, but I knew I had to go
          deeper.
                    (MORE)

                    LIONEL (CONT'D)
Those poor young blokes had cried
out in fear, and no-one was
listening to them. My job was to
give them faith in their voice and
let them know that a friend was
listening. That must ring a few
bells with you, Bertie.

                    BERTIE
You give a very noble account of
yourself.

                    LIONEL
Make inquiries. It's all true.

                    BERTIE
Inquiries have been made! You have
no idea who I have breathing down
my neck. I vouched for you and you
have no credentials.

                    LIONEL
But lots of success! I can't show
you a certificate - there was no
training then. All I know I know by
experience, and that war was some
experience. May plaque says, 'L.
Logue, Speech Defects'. No Dr., no
letters after my name.
       (with mock seriousness)
Lock me in the Tower.

                    BERTIE
I would if I could!

                    LIONEL
On what charge?

                    BERTIE
Fraud! With war looming, you've
saddle this nation with a voiceless
King. Destroyed the happiness of my
family...all for the sake of
ensnaring a star patient you knew
you couldn't possibly assist!

His desperation spills out. He pulls himself out the chair,
striding past Lionel.

Colin Firth as King George VI

Geoffrey Rush as Lionel Logue

Helena Bonham Carter as Queen Elizabeth

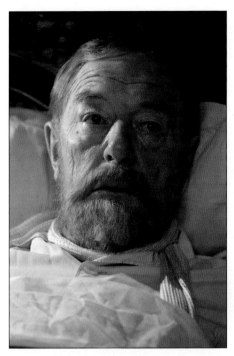

Michael Gambon as King George V

Guy Pearce as King Edward VIII

Timothy Spall as Winston Churchill

Eve Best as Wallis Simpson

Claire Bloom as Queen Mary

Jennifer Ehle as Myrtle Logue

Bertie attempting to make a speech.

Bertie with his wife Elizabeth.

Edward VIII making his abdication speech.

King George VI and his wife Elizabeth listening to the abdication speech.

George VI seeking assistance for his stammer from Lionel Logue.

Lionel Logue, King George VI, and Archbishop Cosmo Lang (Derek Jacobi)

Lionel Logue working with George VI.

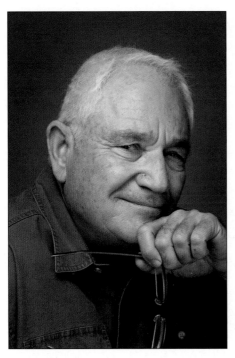

Screenwriter David Seidler

Director Tom Hooper

> BERTIE (CONT'D)
> It'll be like mad King George the
> Third, there'll be Mad King George
> the Stammerer, who let his people
> down so badly in their hour of
> need!

Lionel sits down on the chair of Edward the Confessor.

> BERTIE (CONT'D)
> What're you doing? Get up! You
> can't sit there!

Overlapping-

> LIONEL
> Why not? It's a chair.

> BERTIE
> No, it's not, that is Saint
> Edward's Chair-

> LIONEL
> People have carved their initials
> into it!

> BERTIE
> That chair is the seat on which
> every King and Queen-

> LIONEL
> It's held in place by a large rock!

> BERTIE
> That is the Stone of Scone, you are
> trivialising everything-

> LIONEL
> I don't care. I don't care how many
> Royal arses have sat in this chair-

Overlapping-

> BERTIE
> Listen to me... !

> LIONEL
> Listen to you?! By what right?

> BERTIE
> Divine right, if you must! I'm your
> King!!!

                    LIONEL
Noooo you're not! Told me so
yourself. Said you didn't want it.
So why should I waste my time
listening to you?

                    BERTIE
Because I have a right to be heard!

                    LIONEL
Heard as what?!

                    BERTIE
A man! I HAVE A VOICE!!!

                    LIONEL
          (quietly)
Yes you do. You have such
perseverance, Bertie, you're the
bravest man I know. And you'll make
a bloody good king.

Bertie stares at him.

A familiar voice is heard from the shadows.

                    VOICE
What on earth's going on, Sir?

                    BERTIE
It's all right, Archbishop.

The Archbishop of Canterbury.

                    COSMO LANG
Mr Logue, you should know that I
have found a replacement *English*
specialist with impeccable
credentials. Hence, your services
will no longer be required.

                    BERTIE
I'm sorry?

                    COSMO LANG
Your Majesty's function is to
consult and be advised. You didn't
consult, but you've just been
advised.

                    BERTIE
Now I advise you: in this personal
matter I will make my own decision.

                    COSMO LANG
          My concern is for the head upon
          which I must place the crown.

                    BERTIE
          I appreciate that Archbishop, but
          it's my head!

                    COSMO LANG
          Your humble servant.

Lang turns on his heel and is gone, leaving Bertie shaken,
with both anger, and fear.

                    LIONEL
          Thank you Bertie. Shall we
          rehearse?

Bertie sits in the ceremonial chair once more.

                    LIONEL (CONT'D)
          As soon as you and Elizabeth enter
          the West door, you'll be greeted
          with the hymn "I Was Glad When They
          Said Unto Me." You won't actually
          be that glad, because they sing it
          for a great long time. Then your
          friend the Archbishop will ponce up
          and say, "Sir, is Your Majesty
          willing to take The Oath?" You
          say..

                    BERTIE
          "I am willing".

                    LIONEL
          Course you are! I'll see what it
          sounds like from the cheap seats so
          even your old nanny can hear.
          "Will you govern your peoples of
          Great Britain, Ireland, Canada,
          Australia and New Zealand according
          to their lands and customs?"

                    BERTIE
          "I solemnly promise so do so."

                    LIONEL
          LOUDER! I can't hear you up the
          back.

                    BERTIE
          "I SOLEMNLY PROMISE TO DO SO!"

                    LIONEL
          Very good! "Will you to your power
          cause Law and Justice, in Mercy, to
          be executed in all your
          judgements?"

                    BERTIE
          "I will." "I WILL!"

                    LIONEL
          Then a long bit about upholding the
          faith, rubbish, rubbish, rubbish.
          To which you finally say...

                    BERTIE
          "These things which I have
          herebefore promised, I will perform
          and keep. So help me God."

                    LIONEL
          That's all you have to say. Four
          short responses, kiss the book and
          sign the oath. There you are:
          you're King. Easy.

The faint CLICKING WHIR of a film projector is heard.

79   INT. SCREENING ROOM, BUCKINGHAM PALACE - NEW DAY   79

On the screen: archive - Pathe newsreel footage of the
Coronation.

The Royal Family watches: Bertie, Elizabeth, Lilibet and
Margaret. Cosmo Lang and his assistant are in attendance.
There is a projectionist also.

                    MARGARET ROSE
          You nearly crowned him backwards
          Archbishop!

Lang steps in front of the screen, eager to explain

                    COSMO LANG
          Someone had removed the thread that
          was marking the front of the Crown,
          Sir.

                    BERTIE
          Try not lose the thread,
          Archbishop.

>   LILLIBET
>   (peering around Lang)
>   Archbishop, your missing Papa.

We see Bertie giving two of his responses.

>   ELIZABETH
>   Very good, very good. Archbishop.

>   COSMO LANG
>   Well, I hope Your Majesties are
>   thrilled with the result.

The Coronation footage finishes. The next segment of the
newsreel is entitled "Hitler in Nuremberg!" and shows him
viewing troops doing the goose-step amidst immense crowds. We
then see Hitler's mad eloquence, mesmerizing all.

>   COSMO LANG (CONT'D)
>   (to the projectionist)
>   You can turn that off now.

>   ELIZABETH
>   No, wait, keeping going.

>   LILLIBET
>   Do have a seat, Archbishop.

They watch the footage.

>   LILLIBET
>   What's he saying, Papa?

>   BERTIE
>   I don't know, but he seems to be
>   saying it rather well.

Off the roar of the crowds on the screen.

Bertie's face as he watches Hitler.

80   INT. MEETING ROOM, BUCKINGHAM PALACE - NEW DAY   80

Baldwin enters, looking pale and tired, to see Bertie.

>   BERTIE
>   Good Morning Mr Baldwin.

>   BALDWIN
>   Good Morning your Majesty.
>   Congratulations on your Coronation.
>   It went splendidly.

                    BERTIE
Thank you, Prime Minister. Luckily
I only had to repeat a few short
oaths. I may not be so fortunate in
the future.

                    BALDWIN
Sir, I have asked to see you today
in order to tender my resignation
as Prime Minister.

                    BERTIE
I am so sorry to hear that, Mr
Baldwin.

                    BALDWIN
Neville Chamberlain will take my
place as Prime Minister. It's a
matter of principal. I was
mistaken. I have found it
impossible to believe that there is
any man in the World so lacking in
moral feeling as Hitler, but the
world might be hurled for a second
time into the abyss of destructive
War. Churchill was right all along.
This was always Hitler's intention.
I am only sorry to leave you in
this time of crisis. I am afraid
Sir, your greatest test is yet to
come.

81   INT. LOGUE'S PARLOUR - DAY   81

The Logue family are sat around the wireless.

                    CHAMBERLAIN
I am speaking to you from the
cabinet room of 10 Downing Street.
This morning the British Ambassador
in Berlin handed the German
Government a final note stating
that unless we heard from them by
11 o'clock that they were prepared
at once to withdraw their troops
from Poland, a state of war would
exist between us. I have to tell
you now that no such undertaking
has been received, and that
consequently this country is at war
with Germany.

82   INT. BUCKINGHAM PALACE, BERTIE'S STUDY - DAY   82

3rd September 1939. Bertie, in uniform, is at his desk going
through paperwork. HARDINGE, the King's Private Secretary,
enters briskly.

                    HARDINGE
          At last. Here it is. You are live
          at six. I've timed it at just under
          nine minutes. The wording is fully
          approved. The Prime Minister will
          be joining you for the broadcast
          which will go out live to the
          Nation, the Empire and to our Armed
          Forces.

                    BERTIE
          Get Logue here immediately.

Hardinge exits. Bertie is left contemplating the speech.
Nervous as hell.

83   INT. - LOGUE'S CAR - DAY   83

Laurie drives Logue. Out the window he sees sandbags being
piled round government buildings.

                    LIONEL
          (peering up into the sky)
          Look, there are the barrage
          balloons. They got them up there
          quickly.

An air raid siren is heard.

                    LAURIE
          Should we pull over and find
          shelter?

                    LOGUE
          No, just go straight on. We'll be
          alright.

                                        CUT TO:

84   INT./EXT. LOGUE'S CAR, OUTSIDE BUCKINGHAM PALACE   84

Logue's ID is checked.

85   EXT. QUADRANGLE, BUCKINGHAM PALACE   85

Logue hurries into the Palace. The car pulls away.

86   INT. COATROOM, BUCKINGHAM PALACE   86

Logue hangs up umbrella, coat and gas mask.

87   INT. STAIRCASE, BUCKINGHAM PALACE   87

Logue is met on the stairs by Hardinge who hands him a
speech.

> HARDINGE
> The King's Speech. We have about
> forty minutes until the broadcast.

Lionel hurries up the stairs.

88   INT. BERTIE'S STUDY, BUCKINGHAM PALACE - DAY   88

Bertie (dressed in his naval uniform) and Logue (dressed in
black tie) are rehearsing.

> BERTIE
> (stammering very badly)
> "There may be dark days ahead, and
> w-w-wa..."

> LIONEL
> Try again.

> BERTIE
> "There may be dark days ahead, and
> w-... "

> LIONEL
> Turn the hesitations into pauses,
> and say to yourself, "God save the
> King".

> BERTIE
> I say that continually, but
> apparently no one's listening.

> LIONEL
> Long pauses are good: they add
> solemnity to great occasions.

                    BERTIE
          Then I'm the solemnest king who
          ever lived. Lionel, I can't do
          this!

                    LIONEL
          Bertie, you can do this!

                    BERTIE
          If I am to be King...where is my
          power? May I form a Government,
          levy a tax or declare a war? No!
          Yet I am the seat of all authority.
          Why? Because the Nation believes
          when I speak, I speak for them. Yet
          I cannot speak!

As though none of this had happened:

                    LIONEL
          Let's take it from the top. "In
          this grave hour..."

                    BERTIE
               (hesitates, then)
          "In this grave hour fuck fuck fuck
          perhaps the most fateful in our
          history bugger shit shit (singing)
          I send to every household of my p-p-
          The letter'P' is always difficult.

                    LIONEL
          Bounce onto it 'a-peoples both at
          home and'

                    BERTIE
          "a-peoples both at home and
          overseas,..."

                    LIONEL
          Beaut.

                    BERTIE
               (singing)
          "... this message, doo-dah, doo-
          dah....spoken with the same depth
          of feeling...for each one of you as
          if I were to fuck shit bugger cross
          your threshold and speak to you m-
          my - ..."

                    LIONEL
          In your head, now: "I have a right
          to be bloody well heard!"

               BERTIE
Bloody well heard, bloody well
heard, bloody well heard myself!

               LIONEL
Now Waltz. Move! Get continuous
movement.

               BERTIE
    (waltzing and singing)
"For the second time in the lives
of most of us we are at wa - ..."

Bertie jams and comes to a halt.

               LIONEL
Pause. "we are..." Take a pause.

               BERTIE
I can't do this.

               LIONEL
Bertie, you can do it. Have a look
at the last paragraph.

               ELIZABETH
Bertie...it's time.

Bertie and Lionel glance at each other.

Bertie approaches the door.

He pauses.

Down a long perspective of rooms we see ahead the waiting
microphone.

Like a tunnel. Like Wembley.

Bertie begins the long walk, flanked by his wife and his
speech specialist.

89   INT. STATE ROOMS, BUCKINGHAM PALACE - CONTINUOUS   89

Bertie, Lionel, and Elizabeth walk towards the microphone.

A corgi barks as they approach.

The first room has a large speaker and chairs arranged for
listening to the broadcast. Lang, Prime Minister Neville
Chamberlain and Churchill are in attendance.

                    BERTIE
          Prime Minister. Nice to see you
          again, so soon. Good of you to be
          here, I'm sure you've had rather a
          busy day.

                    CHAMBERLAIN
          Let's hope we have no more
          interruptions from those damned
          sirens, Sir.

                    BERTIE
          Or the wretched dogs.
               (to Churchill)
          Congratulations. First Lord of the
          Admiralty.

                    WINSTON CHURCHILL
          Your Majesty.

                    BERTIE
               (nodding towards the
                recording room)
          The long walk.

Churchill detaches himself from Lang and walks with Bertie.

                    WINSTON CHURCHILL
          Good luck, Sir. I too dread
          this...apparatus. Had a speech
          impediment myself, you know.

                    BERTIE
          I didn't.

                    WINSTON CHURCHILL
          Family secret. Tongue-tied. An
          operation was considered too
          dangerous. I eventually made an
          asset of it.

A moment of silent recognition between the two men.

                    BERTIE
          Thank you, Mr Churchill.

Churchill nods, then goes to his seat, as Bertie passes into
the next room.

                    BERTIE (CONT'D)
          How long, Logue?

                    LIONEL
          Just under three minutes, Sir.

Ahead is the microphone set up on a grand desk in a
beautifully ornate state room.

Next to it is now revealed a stills camera and lights - all
set for a photo op.

Bertie, Logue and Elizabeth, ignoring it, pass right by, turn
a corner and we now see a perspective of much smaller rooms
leading to a microphone framed in a doorway, hung at head
height. A tumble of cables stretch through the rooms.

We pass through two rooms of audio equipment with eight
technicians all wearing black tie, all set for the broadcast.

Bertie's tension builds.

At the door to the broadcasting booth he is met by the BBC's
Wood.

Bertie greets him

> BERTIE
> Mr Wood.

> WOOD
> Good luck, Your Majesty.

Logue, Bertie and Elizabeth enter the booth.

90   INT. BROADCASTING BOOTH - DAY   90

The dreaded BBC microphone, in a surprisingly small room. It
is arranged so Bertie can stand up as he speaks, the way
Logue likes it. The ceiling has been lowered and it has been
decorated in cheerful colours. As a podium for the speech an
old school desk has been propped up on wooden blocks so it's
the right height for Bertie.

Logue immediately opens the window to get the air
circulating.

Bertie says nothing, but goes up and inspects the looming
microphone.

He spreads the fingers of one hand, touches the apparatus
with the little finger, thumb to chin.

> BERTIE
> I am thistle sifter, I have a sieve
> of sifted thistles and a sieve on
> unsifted thistles..

                    ELIZABETH
          Bertie, darling, make sure it's not
          switched on!

                    LIONEL
          Remember the red light will blink
          three times and then I've asked
          them to turn it off, because we
          don't want that evil eye staring at
          you all the way through.

                    ELIZABETH
          I am sure you will be splendid.

                    WOOD
          One minute, sir.

Elizabeth steps back with a wonderful smile as Wood closes
the door, sealing Bertie and Logue in the booth.

                    BERTIE
          No matter how this turns out, I
          don't know how to thank you for
          what you've done.

                    LIONEL
          Knighthood?

They smile.

                    WOOD (O.S.)
          Twenty seconds.

                    LIONEL
          Forget everything else and just say
          it to me. Say it to me, as a
          friend.

The red light in the booth flashes.

The red light flashes for the second time.

Bertie concentrates.

The red light flashes for the third time.

The red light now goes steady red.

Lionel opens his arms wide and mouths, "Breathe!".

On Air.

Bertie's hands begin to shake, the pages of his speech rattle
like dry leaves, his throat muscles constrict, the Adam's
apple bulges, his lips tighten...all the old symptoms
reappear.

Several seconds have elapsed. It seems an eternity.

91   INT. CONTROL ROOM, BBC BROADCASTING HOUSE - DAY   91

The technicians in their suits, ties and scientific looking
white overcoats, wearing bulky headphones, monitoring
daunting banks of valves and dials listen with growing
apprehension to the silence broken only by crackling static.

92   INT. KING'S STUDY/BROADCAST ROOM, BUCKINGHAM PALACE - DAY 92

The tension is more than palpable.

Bertie and Logue stare at each other.

Logue smiles, perfectly calm, totally confident in the man
he's worked with. His confidence is contagious.

Bertie takes a deep breath, lets it out slowly. His throat
muscles relax, his hands steady - all the things he's
practiced.

>   BERTIE
>   In this grave hour, perhaps the
>   most fateful in our history, I send
>   to every household of my peoples,
>   both at home and overseas this
>   message spoken with the same depth
>   of feeling for each one of you as
>   if I were able to cross your
>   threshold and speak to you myself.

His cadence is slow and measured, not flawless, but he does
not stop.

93   INT - STATE ROOMS - DAY   93

In the listening room:

Elizabeth grasps the sides of her chair and then slowly
relaxes as Bertie's calm, measure voice comes over the
speakers.

94   INT./EXT. MONTAGE OF VARIOUS LOCATIONS   94

The assembled dignitaries at Buckingham Palace, Myrtle with
two of the boys, people listening to radios in homes, pubs,
factories. A group of soldiers, including Antony Logue. Queen
Mary sitting in her State Apartments, David and Wallis
listening dolefully in a villa in the South of France, the
crowds assembled outside Buckingham Palace, listening on loud
speakers. Cutting continually back to Bertie as he grows in
confidence

                    BERTIE (V.O. ON RADIO)
For the second time in the lives of
most of us we are at war. Over and
over again we have tried to find a
peaceful way out of the differences
between ourselves and those who are
now our enemies. But it has been in
vain. We have been forced into a
conflict. For we are called, with
our allies, to meet the challenge of
a principle which, if it were to
prevail, would be fatal to any
civilized order in the world. Such a
principle, stripped of all disguise,
is surely the mere primitive
doctrine that might is right. For
the sake of all that we ourselves
hold dear, and of the world's order
and peace, it is unthinkable that we
should refuse to meet the challenge.
It is to this high purpose that I
now call my people at home and my
peoples across the seas, who will
make our cause their own. I ask them
to stand calm and firm, and united
in this time of trial. The task will
be hard. There may be dark days
ahead, and war can no longer be
confined to the battlefield. But we
can only do the right as we see the
right and reverently commit our
cause to God.

95   INT. BROADCASTING BOOTH, BUCKINGHAM PALACE - CONTINUOUS   95

Bertie, in his quiet way is totally in command, and utterly
magnificent. Everyone in the room is awed as he concludes:

                    BERTIE (CONT'D)
If one and all we keep resolutely
faithful to it, then, with God's
help, we shall prevail.

96   INT. STATE ROOMS, BUCKINGHAM PALACE - CONTINUOUS   96

In the listening room we see the elated faces of Elizabeth, Churchill, Lang.

97   INT. CONTROL ROOM, BBC BROADCASTING HOUSE - DAY   97

Technicians break in to spontaneous applause.

98   INT. BROADCASTING BOOTH, BUCKINGHAM PALACE - CONTINUOUS 98

Lionel and Bertie stare at each other.

Silence.

> LIONEL
> That was very good, Bertie.

Lionel closes the window.

> LIONEL (CONT'D)
> You still stammered on the "w".

> BERTIE
> Had to throw in a few so they knew
> it was me.

Wood opens the door.

> WOOD
> Congratulations, your Majesty. A
> true broadcaster.

> BERTIE
> Thank you, Mr Wood.

Bertie and Lionel pass out of the booth to the sounds of applause.

They pause at the desk, which is set up with a microphone.

Bertie sits and has his official photograph taken.

> LIONEL
> Your first war time speech.
> Congratulations.

> BERTIE
> Expect I shall have to do a great
> deal more. Thank you, Logue.

Bertie stands and takes Lionel's hand

                    BERTIE (CONT'D)
          Thank you. My friend.

                    LIONEL
          Thank you... Your Majesty.

99   INT. STATE ROOMS, BUCKINGHAM PALACE - CONTINUOUS   99

Bertie heads towards the listening room.

Elizabeth goes to Bertie and kisses him tenderly on the
cheek.

                    ELIZABETH
              (whispered, emotional)
          I knew you'd be good.

Elizabeth looks at Lionel.

                    ELIZABETH (CONT'D)
          Thank you...
              (for the first time)
          ...Lionel.

                    BERTIE
          Onwards?

Bertie continues on, and is greeted by Lang, Churchill and
Chamberlain.

                    WINSTON CHURCHILL
          Couldn't have said it better
          myself, Sir

The ultimate Churchillian compliment. Lang next.

                    COSMO LANG
          Your Majesty, I'm speechless.

                    CHAMBERLAIN
          Congratulations, Sir

                    BERTIE
          Thank you, Gentlemen.

Bertie sweeps Lillibet into his arms.

                    BERTIE (CONT'D)
          So how was Papa?

                    LILLIBET
          Halting at first, but you got much
          better Papa.

He kisses her.

> BERTIE
> Bless you.
> (picking Margaret up)
> And how about you?

> MARGARET
> You were just splendid, Papa.

> BERTIE
> Of course I was.

Bertie readies himself to step out on to the balcony; waiting crowds are glimpsed through the windows.

Across the room, Bertie's eyes meet Logue's. A brief nod. A moment of recognition.

100   EXT. BALCONY, BUCKINGHAM PALACE - DAY   100

The King, his Queen and their children wave to the crowds, receiving their adulation and love.

Bertie glances upwards.

POV - silver dirigibles hover protectively.

ON THE BALCONY - Bertie and Elizabeth, King and Queen, wave to their people and receive their approbation.

Lionel watches from the shadow.

CARD:

> King George VI made Lionel Logue a Commander of the Royal Victorian Order in 1944.

> This high honour from a grateful King made Lionel part of the only order of chivalry that specifically rewards acts of personal service to the Monarch.

> Lionel was with the King for every wartime speech.

> Through his broadcasts, George VI became a symbol of national resistance.

> Lionel and Bertie remained friends for the rest of their lives.

THE END

CAST AND CREW CREDITS

THE WEINSTEIN COMPANY and UK FILM COUNCIL PRESENT
IN ASSOCIATION WITH MOMENTUM PICTURES, AEGIS FILM FUND
MOLINARE, LONDON FILMNATION ENTERTAINMENT
A SEE-SAW FILMS / BEDLAM PRODUCTION
A FILM BY TOM HOOPER

COLIN FIRTH   GEOFFREY RUSH

"THE KING'S SPEECH"

HELENA BONHAM CARTER   GUY PEARCE   TIMOTHY SPALL DEREK JACOBI
JENNIFER EHLE ANTHONY ANDREWS CLAIRE BLOOM EVE BEST and MICHAEL GAMBON

Directed by	Executive Producers	Production Designer
TOM HOOPER	HARVEY WEINSTEIN	EVE STEWART
	BOB WEINSTEIN	
Produced by		Costumes Designer
IAIN CANNING	Co-producers	JENNY BEAVAN
EMILE SHERMAN	PETER HESLOP	
GARETH UNWIN	SIMON EGAN	Make-up and Hair Designer
		FRANCES HANNON
Screenplay by	Director of Photography	
DAVID SEIDLER	DANNY COHEN BSC	Music Supervisors
		MAGGIE RODFORD
Executive Producers	Composer	
GEOFFREY RUSH	ALEXANDRE DESPLAT	Casting Director
TIM SMITH		NINA GOLD
PAUL BRETT	Film Editor	
MARK FOLIGNO	TARIQ ANWAR	

CAST IN ORDER OF APPEARANCE

King George VI. . . . . COLIN FIRTH
Queen Elizabeth. . HELENA BONHAM CARTER
Archbishop Cosmo Lang . . . . . DEREK JACOBI
Equerry. . . . . ROBERT PORTAL
Private Secretary. . . . . . . RICHARD DIXON
Chauffeur. . . . . PAUL TRUSSELL
BBC Radio Announcer
. . . . ADRIAN SCARBOROUGH
Robert Wood . . . . ANDREW HAVILL
BBC Technician . . . . CHARLES ARMSTRONG
Dr Blandine-Bentham . . . ROGER HAMMOND
Lionel Logue . . . . GEOFFREY RUSH
Laurie Logue . . . . CALUM GITTINS
Myrtle Logue. . . . . JENNIFER EHLE
Valentine Logue . . . DOMINIC APPLEWHITE
Anthony Logue . . . . BEN WIMSETT
Princess Elizabeth . . . . FREYA WILSON
Princess Margaret . . . . . RAMONA MARQUEZ
Theatre Director . . . . DAVID BAMBER
Willie . . . . JAKE HATHAWAY
King George V . . . . MICHAEL GAMBON
King Edward VIII . . . . GUY PEARCE

Lord Wigram . . . . PATRICK RYECART
Nurse . . . . TERESA GALLAGHER
Lord Dawson . . . . SIMON CHANDLER
Queen Mary . . . . CLAIRE BLOOM
Duke of Kent . . . . ORLANDO WELLS
Duke of Gloucester . . . . TIM DOWNIE
Butler . . . . DICK WARD
Wallis Simpson . . . . EVE BEST
Footman . . . . JOHN ALBASINY
Winston Churchill . . . . . . TIMOTHY SPALL
Boy in Regent's Park . . . . DANNY EMES
Stanley Baldwin . . . . . ANTHONY ANDREWS
Steward . . . . JOHN WARNABY
Neville Chamberlain . . . . . ROGER PARROTT

Co-Executive Producers . . . . . DEEPAK SIKKA
                                  LISBETH SAVILL
                                  PHIL HOPE

Associate Producer . . . . CHARLES DORFMAN

Line Producer. . . . . PETER HESLOP

Production Manager. . . . . . . ERICA BENSLY

First Assistant Director . . . MARTIN HARRISON

Supervising Art Director . . . . . DAVID HINDLE

Production Sound Mixer. . . . . JOHN MIDGLEY

Production Coordinator . . . . FIONA GARLAND
Assistant Production Coordinator
. . . . JONATHAN HOUSTON
Director's Assistant . . . . . . FRANCESCA BUDD
Production Runner. . STEFANO MARGARITELLI

Script Supervisor. . . . . . CATHY DOUBLEDAY
Second Assistant Director . . . CHRIS STOALING
Third Assistant Director . . . . . HEIDI GOWER
Floor Runner . . . . DARREN PRICE
Crowd Assistant Director . . . CHARLIE WALLER
Crowd Assistant Director (Yorkshire)
. . . . JULIE HESKIN

Production Accountant
. . . . MARILYN GOLDSWORTHY
First Assistant Accountant . . . . . PETER CLARK
Assistant Accountant . . . . MATTHEW LAWSON

Dialect Coach. . . . . NEIL SWAIN
Casting Assistant . . . . KHARMEL COCHRANE
Choreographer . . . . . . SCARLETT MACKMIN

Logue Family Consultant . . . . . MARK LOGUE
Historical Advisor . . . . HUGO VICKERS
Military & Ceremonial Advisor
. . . . ALASTAIR BRUCE
Military Advisor. . . . . EDWIN FIELD

A Camera / Steadicam Operator
. . . . ZAC NICHOLSON
A Camera Focus Puller . . . . . PETER BYRNE
A Camera Clapper Loader. . . . ABIGAIL CATTO
B Camera Operator . . . . . . DANNY COHEN
B Camera Focus Puller. . . . . . . LEIGH GOLD
B Camera Clapper Loader . . . MAX GLICKMAN
Video Playback Operator . . . . . LIZZIE KELLY
Camera Trainee. . . . . ELLIOT DUPUY

A Camera Grip . . . . ALEX MOTT
B Camera Grip . . . . SIMON FOGG

Gaffer . . . . PAUL MCGEACHAN
Best Boy . . . . WILL KENDAL
Electricians. . . . . TOM HYDE

SEAN DAVIS
ALAN FRASER
DANNY GRIFFITHS
Electrical Rigger . . . . GUY COPE
Airstar Head Technician . . . . IAIN YOUNG
Airstar Lead Technician. . . MARC WOODCOCK

Sound Maintenance. . . . . . MIKE REARDON
Cable / 3rd Persons . . . . . CHARLOTTE GREY
JOE CAREY

Art Director . . . . LEON MCCARTHY
Set Decorator . . . . JUDY FARR
Production Buyer . . . . CORINA FLOYD

Art Department Coordinator. . . . JULIA CASTLE
Standby Art Director . . . . . NETTY CHAPMAN
Graphic Designer . . . . AMY MERRY
Art Department Assistant . . . CAMISE OLDFIELD
Storyboard Artist . . . . . DOUGLAS INGRAM
Art Department Runners . . REBECCA WALKER
EVA ONSRUD
EMMA WEAVER

Prop Master . . . . BRUCE BIGG
Dressing Propman / Storeman
. . . . WARREN STICKLEY
Dressing Propmen . . . . . MICHAEL FLEMING
PETER HASLER
Standby Propmen . . . . MITCH NICLAS
ANDY FORREST

Assistant Costume Designers . . . ALISON BEARD
SALLY TURNER
Costume Supervisor. . . . . . MARCO SCOTTI
Costume Standbys . . . . . . DAVID OTZEN
KATHERINE GREENACRE
Costume Assistant. . . JENNA MCGRANAGHAN

Hair & Make-up Artists . . . . NANA FISCHER
CARMEL JACKSON
CHRISTINE WHITNEY
PAUL GOOCH
Hair & Make-up Trainee. . . . . . CLARICE GILL

Location Managers. . . . . . . JAMIE LENGYEL
DAVID BRODER
Assistant Location Managers. . . REBECCA DAVIS
TOM ASQUITH
Unit Manager. . . . . DAVE BELL
Location Assistants . . . . . . LINDSEY POWELL
PAUL TOMLINSON
Location Scout . . . . . CAMILLA STEPHENSON

Construction Manager . . . . . ALAN CHESTERS
Chargehand Carpenter . . . . JO HAWTHORNE
Carpenters . . . . LEIGH CHESTERS
SIMON ROBILLIARD
Supervising Painter. . . . . . . JOHN ROBERTS
Scenic Painter . . . . DAVID MEARS
Painter . . . . GEORGE ROBERTS
Stagehand . . . . MICHAEL WEBB
Construction Driver. . . . . . . BILLY PIDGLEY

Standby Carpenter. . . . . DAVID 'NED' KELLY
Standby Painter . . . . . HENRY GALLAGHER
Standby Rigger . . . . JOHN HANKS

Special Effects Supervisor . . . . . MARK HOLT
Special Effects Floor Supervisor
. . . . JAMIE WEGUELIN
Special Effects Senior Technician
. . . . PATRICK O'SULLIVAN

Public Relations . . DDA PUBLIC RELATIONS LTD
Unit Publicist . . . . EMMA DAVIE
Stills Photographer . . . . . LAURIE SPARHAM
EPK. . . . . SPECIAL TREATS

King George VI Stand-in. . . . . ROY BORRETT
Lionel Logue Stand-in . . . STEVEN MORPHEW
Queen Elizabeth Stand-in. . HELEN SLAYMAKER
Utility Stand-in . . . . . . RICHARD MANLOVE

Transport Captain. . . . . SIMON JONES
Driver to Mr Hooper . . DAVID O'DONOGHUE
Driver to Mr Firth. . . . . TONY WADSWORTH
Driver to Mr Rush . . . . LEE ISGAR
Driver to Ms Bonham Carter. . HARRY TAYLOR
Driver to Mr Pearce . . . . . DANNY JARMAN
Unit Drivers. . . . . DEBBIE BRYANT
STEVE PIROLLI
Minibus Drivers . . . . JOHN AYRES
MARK BELLETT

Catering by . . PREMIER CATERERS LIMITED
Proprietor. . . . . PETER TITTERELL
Catering Manager. . . . . KEVIN CHAMBERLIN
Chef. . . . . DAVE HAYBALL
Catering Assistants . . . . CHRISTINE PERRETT
WILL MCCORD
JEREMY SELLICK

Health & Safety Officers. . . . . . . MIKE RYAN
BARRY MAY-LEYBOURNE
JOHN DALTON

Unit Nurse . . . . CARRIE JOHNSON

2nd Unit Director of Photography
. . . . MARTIN KENZIE
2nd Unit First Assistant Director . . GUY HEELEY
2nd Unit Crowd Second Assistant Director
. . . . CHARLIE REED
2nd Unit Third Assistant Directors
. . . . TOM BREWSTER
ANDY MANNION
LIAM LOCK
2nd Unit Focus Pullers . . . . . SHAUN COBLEY
DAVID COZENS
OLIVER LONCRAINE
NATHAN MANN
BEN WILSON

2nd Unit Clapper Loaders
. . . . DAVE CHURCHYARD
CHLOE THOMSON
2nd Unit Camera Trainee . . . . . WILL MORRIS

2nd Unit Video Playback Operators
. . . . MARTYN CULPAN
GUY MCCORMACK
2nd Unit Grips. . . . . JODY KNIGHT
DEAN MORRIS
GARY HUTCHINGS
2nd Unit Sound Mixer . . . . . MARTIN SEELEY
2nd Unit Sound Assistant . DASH MASON-MALIK

2nd Unit Costume Assistants
LUCILLE ACEVEDO-JONES • TIM ASLAM •
ANN CARTWRIGHT • JANINE CUNLIFFE •
JASON GILL • LINDA O'REILLY • FOLA
SOLANKE • VANESSA WOOLGAR

2nd Unit Hair & Make-up Artists
SHARON O'BRIEN • HELEN BARRETT •
CATHY BURCZAK • KAREN COHEN •
SARAH GRISPO • MAUREEN HETHERING-
TON • LISA PICKERING • LOULIA SHEPPARD

Post Production Supervisor. . . . . . . EMMA ZEE
Post Production Coordinator . . SIOBHAN BOYES
Delivery Paperwork Coordinator
. . . . SARAH PARFITT
Post Production Accountant . . PETER EARDLEY

Sound Post Production by . . . . . . BOOM POST
Supervising Sound Editor . . . . . LEE WALPOLE

Assistant Sound Editor . . . . PHILIP CLEMENTS
Sound Effects Editors. . CATHERINE HODGSON
                                 JIM GODDARD
Dialogue Editors. . . . . . . ANDRE SCHMIDT
                             MATT SKELDING
Assistant Dialogue Editor . . . VIRGINIA THORN
Assistant Sound Editor . . . PHILIP CLEMENTS
Foley Recordist & Editor. . CATHERINE THOMAS
Foley Artists. . . . . PETER BURGIS
                            ANDI DERRICK
Re-recording Mixer . . . . . . PAUL HAMBLIN
ADR & Assistant Re-recording Mixer
. . . . FORBES NOONAN
Additional Re-recording Mixer . . MARTIN JENSEN

ADR (Australia). . SOUND FIRM, MELBOURNE
ADR (London) . . . . PEPPER, LONDON
ADR (New York) . . . . . SOUND ONE, NYC
ADR (Hawaii). . . . . AUDIO IMAGES, KAUAI

Digital Intermediate by . . MOLINARE, LONDON
Post Production Manager . . . . . . ALAN PRITT
Digital Intermediate Conform Editors
. . . . STEVE KNIGHT
           GEMMA TOWNSEND
           FRANCOIS KAMFFER
              JAMIE WELSH

Colourist . . . . GARETH SPENSLEY

On-line Editor . . . . CONNAN MCSTAY
Digital Film Supervisor . . . . . . MATT JAMES
Digital Film Technicians . . . . TIM DREWETT
. . . . MIKE ANDREWS
Digital Film Consultant. . . . . SOREN KLOCH
Film Consultant . . . . LEN BROWN

VFX Editor. . . . . TONY TROMPETTO

VFX by. . . . . MOLINARE, LONDON

VFX Supervisor / Producer. . . . TOM HORTON
VFX Line Producer . . . . FAWNDA DENHAM
VFX Production Coordinator
. . . . DUNCAN HOLLAND
Head of Production. . . . . SAL URMEJI
On-set VFX Supervisor . . . . PHILIP ATTFIELD
Additional on-set VFX Supervision
. . . . NEIL CUNNINGHAM
2D Lead . . . . NIK MARTIN
Senior 2D Artists . . . . SIMON KILROE
               ANTHONY WEBB
2D Artists . . . . RICK MCMAHON

           ALASDAIR MCNEIL
           JOHN HARDWICK
           MARC HUTCHINGS
           ZISSIS PAPATZIKIS
           TERENCE ALVARES
              JOSS FLORES
Matte Painters . . . . SERDAR SIMGA
         AUDRIUS URBONAVICIUS
Senior CG Artist . . . . . . JULIAN JOHNSON
VFX Editor. . . . . COLLETTE NUNES
VFX Data Ops . . . . LIAM TULLY

For Pixion

CG Supervisor . . . . VIRAL THAKKAR
CG Artists. . . . . NEHA
                         ANTRA
Match Mover . . . . SOHIL SHAIK
2D Supervisor. . RANADHEER REDDY (RANA)
2D Lead . . . . SANJIV NAIK

2D Artists . . . . SANKET GUNE
           PRATIK KALBENDE
                 ABHIJIT
               SREEKANTH
              ANIL RAWAT
           INDRESH TIWARI
             SAARIKA ALI
              ASHOK UCHIL
            ARUN MENDON
          ABHIMAN NIMAAN
          DEBASHISH BORA
            PRATIK DUBEY
           RITU CHOURASIA

Music Composed and Conducted by
. . . . ALEXANDRE DESPLAT

Piano Solo . . . . DAVE ARCH

Orchestra Leader / Violin Solos. . THOMAS BOWES

Music Recorded and Mixed at
. . . . . . ABBEY ROAD STUDIOS, LONDON

Score Recorded and Mixed by . . . PETE COBBIN

Source Music Recorded and Mixed by
. . . . ANDREW DUDMAN

Assisted by . . . . SAM OKELL
             JOHN BARRETT

Score Orchestra Contractor . . ISOBEL GRIFFITHS

Assistant Orchestra Contractor. . LUCY WHALLEY
Supervising Music Editor . . GERARD MCCANN
Music Editor . . . . PETER CLARKE

Music Orchestrated by. . JEAN-PASCAL BEINTUS
. . . . ALEXANDRE DESPLAT

Score Music Preparation . . . . . JILL STREETER
Score Coordinator for Composer
. . . . XAVIER FORCIOLI

Assistant Music Supervisor . . . . . HELEN YATES

Source Music
Conducted by . . . . TERRY DAVIES

Music Performed by
. . THE LONDON SYMPHONY ORCHESTRA
Soloists . . . . STEVE OSBORNE
ANDREW MARRINER
Leader . . . . CARMINE LAURI

Music Librarian . . . . IRYNA KISZKO

Music Services provided by Air-Edel Associates
Limited

Animal Handlers. . . ANIMALS O'KAY LIMITED
Horse Handlers. . ATKINSON ACTION HORSES
THE DEVIL'S HORSEMEN
Armourer. . . . . BAPTY AND CO
Camera Equipment . . . TAKE 2 FILMS LIMITED
Lighting Equipment
. . . . . . ARRI LIGHTING RENTAL LIMITED
Film Stock
. . FUJIFILM MOTION PICTURE FILM LIMITED
Color by . . . . DELUXE
Post Production Script . . . . . . SAPEX SCRIPTS
Location Facilities. . MOVIE MAKERS FACILITIES
Transport. . . PRODUCTION DRIVERS GUILD
LAYS INTERNATIONAL
MEDIA COACHES
SPACON
Health & Safety
. . . . . . EUROSAFETY (DDA FIRE) LIMITED
Medical Services (London)
. . . . ON SET MEDICAL LIMITED
Medical Services (Yorkshire)
. . . . FD TRAINING LIMITED
Walkie Talkies . . . . . . WAVEVEND LIMITED
Script Clearances & Archive Research by
. . . . RUTH HALLIDAY
OF THE CLEARING HOUSE

Legal Services . . . . OLSWANG
Banking Services . . . . COUTTS
Auditor. . MOSES NYACHAE OF RSM TENON
Insurance Broker . . . . PAUL CABLE OF MEDIA
AND ENTERTAINMENT
INSURANCE SERVICES LIMITED
Completion Guarantor. . . . . . FILM FINANCES
International Sales Agent
. . . . . . FILMNATION ENTERTAINMENT
GLEN BASNER
ALISON COHEN

For See-Saw Films Ltd
Production Executive (UK)
. . . . KATHERINE BRIDLE
Production Executive (AUS)
. . . . SIMONE NICHOLSON
Legal and Business Affairs . . . . BARRY SECHOS
Accountant. . . . . HELEN WONG

For Bedlam Productions Ltd
Office Manager . . . . SAMANTHA ROBINSON
Company Accountant . . . . LISA JONES
Production Assistant. . . . . . WILL EMSWORTH
On behalf of Aegis Film Fund Limited
Commercial Manager. . ELIZABETH BLACKLEDGE
Office Executive . . . . . . ANNA BRAZINOVA
Production Accountant . . . . . . ISABEL CHICK
Head of Administration . . . . CLARE KENNEDY
Director of Film Finance . . . . ANNE SHEEHAN
Commercial Director . . . . JAMES SWARBRICK

For The Weinstein Company
Senior Vice President, Production & Development
. . . . BEN FAMIGLIETTI
Senior Vice President, Business Affairs & Acquisitions
. . . . MICHAL PODALL STEINBERG

For Momentum Pictures
President. . . . . CHARLES LAYTON
President of International Distribution
. . . . XAVIER MARCHAND
SVP of Acquisitions, Worldwide
. . . . ROBERT WALAK
Director of Legal & Business Affairs, Europe
. . . . SPYRO MARKESINIS

For UK Film Council
Head of Premiere Fund . . . . . SALLY CAPLAN
Head of Business Affairs . . . . WILL EVANS
Head of Production Finance . . VINCE HOLDEN
Head of Production . . . . . FIONA MORHAM

For Molinare, London
Director . . . . STEVE MILNE
Film Executive . . . . M J MCMAHON

All Classical Repertoire Licensed courtesy of
Resonant Music (1) Limited Partners

'The Marriage of Figaro' Overture
Composed by Wolfgang Amadeus Mozart

'Symphony No.7 in A Major' Op.92 Allegretto
Composed by Ludwig van Beethoven

Piano Concerto No.5 'Emperor' 2nd Movement
Composed Ludwig van Beethoven

'Requiem' 2nd Movement
Composed by Johannes Brahms

Clarinet Concerto 1st Movement
Composed by Wolfgang Amadeus Mozart

'Who's Been Polishing The Sun'
Written by Noel Gay
Performed by Ambrose and His Orchestra
Published by Richard Armitage Ltd
Master courtesy of Decca Music Group Ltd.
Under licence from Universal Music Operations Ltd.

'Shout for Happiness'
Written by Jack Hart and Tom Blight
Performed by Al Bowlly
Published by Campbell Connelly & Co Ltd.
Master courtesy of Past Perfect Vintage Music, UK
Under licence from Universal Music Operations Ltd.

'I Love You Truly'
Written by Carrie Jacobs Bond and Irving King
Performed by Al Bowlly
Published by Campbell Connelly & Co Ltd.
Master courtesy of Decca Music Group Ltd.
Under licence from Universal Music Operations Ltd.

Film & Audio Archive Footage supplied by ITN
Source • ITN Source/Reuters • ITN Source/Images
of War • British Pathé • British Movietone News •
BBC Motion Gallery

Photographs / Graphics / Images used with permission of Unilever • Penguin Group (USA) Ltd

Initially developed with Joan Lane of Wild Thyme
Productions

Developed and Supported by Richard Price of
RPTA

Developed with Buckland Productions and
Charles Dorfman

With Special Thanks to
The Logue Family • The BBC for loan of museum
pieces and help and advice • The British Vintage
Wireless and Television Museum • The Projected
Picture Trust • Dunhill for loan of archive pieces •
Asprey for loan of jewellery pieces • John Trenouth &
John Thompson • Elliott Levin • Fred Specktor •
Doug MacLaren • Paul Lyon-Maris • Sally Long-Innes
• Nicki Van Gelder • Hugo Young • Boaty Boatright •
Pippa Markham • Chris Andrews • James Shirras • Neil
Calder • Lynda Mamy • Laura Engel • Alice Dunne •
Andrew Mackie • Richard Payten • Matt Brodlie •
Mike Selwyn • Peter Garner • Ben Townley • Caroline
Sherman • Brian & Gene Sherman • Scott Canning •
Alexis King • John Canning • Patricia Porter •
Christopher & Anne Unwin • Albert Martinez-Martin
• Sarah Caughey • Christos Michaels • Rebecca Pick •
Andrew Cripps • Nigel Whitehouse • Paul Renney •
Nigel Bennet • Philip Ziegler • Rhodri Thomas •
Tariq Mirza • Alice Clough • Clare Hardwick • Peter
Nichols • Kathryn Nichols • Robert Stromberg •
Derek Bird • Melinka Thompson-Godoy • Brad
Kalinoski • Ben Sumner • Cyntia Buell • Kelly Fischer
• Steve Dellerson • Migs Rustia • Paul Stemmer •

With Thanks to
Movie Makers • Cobella Akqa Hair Salon,
Kensington • Ray Marston Wig Studio • Crème de la
Mer • Dermologica • Carpet Fitters at Ely Cathedral
• Mills Carpets • Adrian Benson • Andrew
Whitehead • Andrew Jennings • Christian Biggs •
Jamie Craven • Ryan Labourn • Fred Porter at 33
Portland Place • Dr Alastair Niven • Ely Cathedral •
The Royal Parks • Andy Pavord and Southwark Film
Office • Nigel Gale and Westminster Events • The
Foreign and Commonwealth Office • The Bradford
Bulls • Leeds United Football Club • Knebworth
House • Englefield House • Cumberland Lodge •
Queen Street Mill Textile Museum • The Drapers
Company • RAF Halton House • Film London •
Van Cleef & Arpels •

The director would like to thank his parents, Meredith and Richard Hooper, for their involvement in the making of this film. He dedicates "The King's Speech" to the memory of his architect grandfather, Edwin Morris Hooper, a navigator in Bomber Command, killed on active service 16 February 1942, aged thirty years.

Made at Elstree Studios, England

Filmed on location in London

Filmed by kind permission of The Greenwich Foundation for the Old Royal Naval College

Filmed at Hatfield House, Hertfordshire, UK

This film is based on true events. However, certain details, dialogue, scenes and characters have been invented or adapted in the process of dramatisation of the film.

No animals were harmed in the making of this film.

All Rights Reserved.

Made with the support of the National Lottery through the UK Film Council's Development Fund and Premiere Fund

ABOUT THE FILMMAKERS

DAVID SEIDLER (Screenplay by) A Londoner by birth, he developed a profound childhood stutter. As a result, George VI, the stammering King who had to speak, became a boyhood hero, role model, and inspiration for this film.

Commencing with writing dubbing scripts for *Godzilla the Monster* movies, and taking time out to work as Political Advisor to the Prime Minister of Fiji, Seidler has sustained an extensive career with twenty credits to his name including: *Tucker, The Man and His Dream,* starring Jeff Bridges, Joan Allen, and Martin Landau, directed by Francis Coppola; *Malice in Wonderland*, Elizabeth Taylor's return role after a long hiatus, co-starring Jane Alexander—and projects developed for Bruce Willis, Jane Fonda, and Kirk and Michael Douglas.

Nominated for Writing Achievement by the Writers' Guild of America three times: winning for *Onassis, The Richest Man in the World,* with Raul Julia, Anthony Quinn, and Jane Seymour (who won an Emmy for her portrayal of Maria Callas); nominated for *My Father, My Son,* with Keith Carradine and Karl Malden; and *By Dawn's Early Light,* with Richard Crenna.

He has also written three animated features, including *Quest for Camelot* (aka "*The Magic Sword*"), and has lectured at universities in Milan, Rome, and the American Film Institute in Los Angeles.

TOM HOOPER (Director) Tom Hooper's most recent film *The Damned United* starred Michael Sheen as the legendary English football manager Brian Clough. *The Damned United* was nominated by the South Bank Show Awards for best British film and premiered at the Toronto Film Festival. This Sony Pictures/BBC Film, written by Peter Morgan, was based on the novel by David Peace. Tom Hooper has had an unprecedented run of success at the Golden Globes, winning the Golden Globe for best movie or mini-series made for television three years in a row (2007/8/9). His starring actors and actresses have won Golden Globes for their performances three years running. Tom Hooper's *John Adams,* starring Paul Giamatti and Laura Linney, won four Golden Globes and thirteen Emmys—the most Emmys ever awarded to a programme in one year in US television history. Based on the bestselling Pulitzer prize–winning biography by David McCullough, *John*

Adams tells the story of the American Revolution through the eyes of the second president. Hooper directed all nine hours of the mini-series, executive produced by Tom Hanks and Gary Goetzman for HBO. Tom Hooper's *Longford*, about Lord Longford's relationship with the "Moors Murderer" Myra Hindley, won Golden Globes for Jim Broadbent, Samantha Morton, and for best TV film. It was written by Peter Morgan for HBO/Channel 4. Hooper won the Emmy award for directing *Elizabeth I*, starring Helen Mirren and Jeremy Irons. The HBO/Channel 4 miniseries won three Golden Globes and nine Emmy Awards, including Outstanding Miniseries and best actress for Helen Mirrren. Hooper was nominated for a Best Director Emmy for helming the revival of ITV's *Prime Suspect—The Last Witness*, starring Helen Mirren. He directed Hilary Swank and Chiwetel Ejiofor in the BAFTA-nominated film *Red Dust*. Hooper's TV work also includes *Daniel Deronda*, which won the Best Miniseries award at the 2003 Banff TV Festival; *Love in a Cold Climate*, for which Alan Bates was BAFTA nominated; and the multi-award-winning ITV comedy drama *Cold Feet*. For two years running Hooper directed the one-hour specials that won *Eastenders* the BAFTA for best soap. He wrote, directed, and produced the short film *Painted Faces* at age 18, which premiered at the London Film Festival, was released theatrically, and shown on Channel 4. At Oxford University he directed theatre productions with contemporaries Kate Beckinsale and Emily Mortimer, and directed his first TV commercials. 37-year-old Hooper's first film *Runaway Dog* was made at age 13 on a clockwork 16mm Bolex camera using 100 feet of film.

THE WEINSTEIN COMPANY AND UK FILM COUNCIL PRESENT IN ASSOCIATION WITH MOMENTUM PICTURES, AEGIS FILM FUND, MOLINARE, LONDON FILMNATION ENTERTAINMENT, A SEE SAW FILMS/BEDLAM PRODUCTION

A FILM BY TOM HOOPER COLIN FIRTH GEOFFREY RUSH "THE KING'S SPEECH" HELENA BONHAM CARTER GUY PEARCE TIMOTHY SPALL DEREK JACOBI JENNIFER EHLE and MICHAEL GAMBON CASTING DIRECTOR NINA GOLD

MUSIC SUPERVISOR MAGGIE RODFORD MAKE UP/HAIR DESIGNER FRANCES HANNON COSTUME DESIGNER JENNY BEAVAN PRODUCTION DESIGNER EVE STEWART FILM EDITOR TARIQ ANWAR COMPOSER ALEXANDRE DESPLAT DIRECTOR OF PHOTOGRAPHY DANNY COHEN BSC CO-PRODUCERS PETER HESLOP SIMON EGAN

EXECUTIVE PRODUCERS GEOFFREY RUSH TIM SMITH PAUL BRETT MARK FOLIGNO HARVEY WEINSTEIN BOB WEINSTEIN SCREENPLAY BY DAVID SEIDLER PRODUCED BY IAIN CANNING EMILE SHERMAN GARETH UNWIN DIRECTED BY TOM HOOPER

RESTRICTED R®
UNDER 17 REQUIRES ACCOMPANYING
PARENT OR ADULT GUARDIAN
SOME LANGUAGE

See Saw

bedlam productions ltd

MOLINARE

DOLBY DIGITAL IN SELECTED THEATRES

AEGIS FILM FUND

UK FILM COUNCIL LOTTERY FUNDED

http://kingsspeech.com